SAN FRANCISCO

The Essential Guide to the
Golden Gate City

MARLENE GOLDMAN

MAPS BY DAVID LINDROTH INC.

ILLUSTRATED BY
KERREN BARBAS STECKLER

PETER PAUPER PRESS, INC.
WHITE PLAINS, NEW YORK

IN LOVING MEMORY OF JACKIE

THANKS

*To Panos for his inspiration and for enduring
all my late nights while getting this done.*

*To my father for introducing me to San Francisco and to my
family and friends in New York for understanding
when I wanted to make it my home.*

*To my editor Suzanne for her patience in editing
this book while I roamed the world.*

To Kurt and to my friends at Funky Door Yoga and KUSF.

*To my cat Joe-Joe for keeping me company while writing
(and not sitting on my keyboard during crucial deadlines).*

Illustrations copyright © 2007 Kerren Barbas Steckler
Maps © 2007 David Lindroth Inc.

Designed by Heather Zschock

Copyright © 2007
Peter Pauper Press, Inc.
202 Mamaroneck Avenue
White Plains, NY 10601
All rights reserved
ISBN 978-1-59359-867-9
Printed in Hong Kong
7 6 5 4 3

Visit us at www.peterpauper.com

THE LITTLE
BLACK BOOK OF
SAN
FRANCISCO

CONTENTS

INTRODUCTION

San Francisco is a city of icons. The Golden Gate Bridge enveloped in a mantle of fog. Cable cars clanging up and down precipitous slopes. Wharf vendors dishing out creamy clam chowder. But the city is much more than postcard clichés. Embraced by the Pacific Ocean and the San Francisco Bay, it boasts one of the world's most stunning urban settings. Its charms brighten hilltops, punctuate the waterfront, and surprise passersby along colorful streets. San Francisco packs its treasures into a compact, seven-by-seven mile area. Even in this small space, the "Golden Gate City" is a patchwork of distinct neighborhoods that are wonderfully diverse. A dynamic lifestyle is what binds them together. Locals love nothing more than to get outdoors, whether for windsurfing under the Golden Gate, walking their dogs through neighborhood parks, or sipping lattes at sidewalk cafés. And nearly 50 years after their city's flower power hippie heyday, San Franciscans remain overwhelmingly tolerant, left-leaning, and politically and socially active. The best way to explore San Francisco is to wander its streets, often made challenging by hills, some so steep they have embedded stairways. This book offers a sampling of the city's highlights, from downtown to the outer reaches, the Bay to the Pacific, world-class museums to funky shops, exotic restaurants to vibrant nightlife . . . all integral to one definition of what is San Francisco.

HOW TO USE THIS GUIDE

You'll find foldout maps by neighborhood with color-coded numbers corresponding to places mentioned in the text. **Red** symbols indicate **Places to See**: landmarks and arts & entertainment. **Blue** symbols indicate **Places to Eat & Drink**: restaurants, cafés, bars, and nightlife. Orange symbols show Where to Shop. Green symbols indicate Where to Stay. Color-coded "**Kids**" references relate to places especially geared to children. Some listings appear in bold but are not mapped. Addresses, phone numbers, and Web sites are included for your travel-planning convenience.

Here are our keys for restaurant and hotel costs:

Restaurants
Cost of an appetizer and main course without drinks
($)   Up to $25
($$) $25–$45
($$$) $45 and up

Hotels
Cost per night
($) $50–$125
($$) $125–$250
($$$) $250 and up

GETTING TO SAN FRANCISCO

San Francisco International Airport (SFO) *(www.flysfo.com)* is just 14 miles south of the city center. Shuttle vans and taxis provide door-to-door drop-off in the city. Visitors can also hop on an **AirTrain** from the airport terminal to the airport **BART (Bay Area Rapid Transit)** *(www.bart.gov)* station. BART deposits passengers at various stops along Market Street downtown, though most hotels will still be a cab or bus ride away. The **Airporter** bus heads downtown as well. **SamTrans** buses serve downtown San Francisco as well as San Mateo County to the south of the city. **Oakland International Airport (OAK)** *(www.flyoakland.com)* is several miles south of downtown Oakland in the East Bay. **AirBART** shuttle buses run between the airport and the Oakland Coliseum BART stations. From here, you can catch a train to downtown San Francisco. Door-to-door shuttle vans also run the route. **Mineta San José International Airport (SJC)** *(www.sjc.org)*, at the southern end of the Bay, is about an hour from San Francisco. Catch the **Caltrain** *(www.caltrain.com)* from here; it runs to the southern edge of San Francisco. The **Airport Flyer** bus connects to the Santa Clara Caltrain Station.

GETTING AROUND THE CITY

San Francisco is one of California's best "on-foot" cities, though the hills can be tough going and many of its attractions are spread out. One option is to **rent a car**, but driving is tricky here, with the steep hills, one-way streets, and limited parking. If you do drive, remember when parking to curb your front wheels. When parking uphill, turn the wheels out toward the street; downhill, turn the wheels into the curb. Always set the parking brake. **Renting a bicycle** is another option, though cyclists will find some streets a fierce uphill challenge or an alarming downhill slide. Fortunately, there are routes that avoid the steeper slopes, making cycling a fun choice *(www.sfbike.org)*. Even a quick day ride over the Golden Gate Bridge is memorable. Every last Friday of the month, San Francisco bike riders converge on Market Street for "Critical Mass," a take-back-the-streets celebration of cycling. The riders pack three or four city blocks at the end of rush hour. **Rollerbladers** have several skate areas to choose from, including Crissy Field and Golden Gate Park on Sundays when traffic is blocked. Or join the Midnight Rollers *(www.cora.org)* for a 12-mile group skate through the city every Friday night.

MUNI *(415-673-6864, www.sfmuni.com)*, San Francisco's municipal transit agency, operates more than 30 bus lines (many include electric buses) and subway service. MUNI maps are available at drugstores, bookstores, and the **San Francisco Visitor Information Center** *(900 Market St., 415-391-2000, www.onlyinsanfrancisco.org) (see page 63)*. You'll also find them hanging at many bus stops and metro stations. MUNI offers night "Owl" service on some lines, making it possible to get around 24 hours a day. Exact change is required. MUNI passports, good for unlimited rides on cable cars, streetcars, and buses, are available for one, three, or seven consecutive days. These money-saving passes are available at many businesses and at the MUNI kiosk at Powell and Market.

The **BART (Bay Area Rapid Transit)** *(415-989-2278, www.bart.gov)* system is a fast and convenient subway system linking San Francisco with the East Bay. BART services Oakland, Berkeley, and points farther east and south. BART also runs to the San Francisco International Airport and the Oakland International Airport. BART service ends around midnight for many stations; you can check exact times using its Quick Planner *(www.bart.gov)*. In San Francisco, BART trains run underground along Market Street. **Caltrain** *(800-660-4287, www.caltrain.com)* connects San Francisco with points south, including San José.

Golden Gate Bridge, Highway, and Transportation District *(415-455-2000, www.goldengate.org)* operates bus and ferry service in San Francisco and Marin and parts of Sonoma counties. Buses run to Sausalito, Mill Valley, Tiburon, Santa Rosa, and other communities. Ferries, which depart from the Ferry Building at the foot of Market Street, head to Larkspur and Sausalito.

Alcatraz Cruises *(Pier 33, 415-981-ROCK or 415-981-7625, www.alcatrazcruises.com)* is the official provider of ferry transportation and visitor services to **Alcatraz Island** *(see page 26)*. The **Blue & Gold Fleet** *(415-705-5555, www.blueandgoldfleet.com)* takes passengers to Angel Island and other destinations. It also offers bus tours of the Sonoma-Napa wine region, Monterey/Carmel, Yosemite, and more. One-hour Bay cruises depart from Pier 41, Fisherman's Wharf. **Red and White Fleet** *(415-673-2900, www.redandwhite.com)* offers cruises from Pier 43 1/2. The **Alameda/Oakland Ferry** *(510-749-5972, www.eastbayferry.com)* departs daily from Pier 39 and from the Ferry Building on Embarcadero at the foot of Market.

CityPass *(888-330-5008, www.citypass.com)* offers discount admission to top attractions, a Bay cruise, and a seven-day passport providing unlimited transportation on cable cars, F-line streetcars, and all Muni services.

For more visitors information, contact the **San Francisco Convention & Visitors Bureau** *(900 Market St., 415-391-2000, www.onlyinsanfrancisco.com) (see page 63)*.

★ CABLE CARS AND STREETCARS

TOP PICK!

San Francisco's historic rail transit system, comprising its world-famous **cable cars** (*www.sfcablecar.com*) and **streetcars** (*www.streetcar.org*), is an attraction itself. But what's the difference?

According to the Market Street Railway preservation organization, "If it runs on steel rails with a wire overhead and a pole touching the wire, it's a **streetcar**. If it runs on steel rails with an open slot between them, and no overhead wires, it's a **cable car**." Cable cars are pulled along on rails by a moving cable beneath the street. The cable is guided by a pulley system at the main powerhouse, where huge electric motor-driven wheels maintain a constant speed of 9.5 miles per hour. **Streetcars** (or "trams" or "trolleys") also run on rails, but draw power from an overhead electric wire.

Cable cars were introduced here more than 130 years ago. At that time, a number of international cities had cable cars. Today, San Francisco's are the last in the world. Three lines operate daily:

- The **Powell-Hyde line** goes from Powell and Market over Nob Hill and Russian Hill to Hyde and Beach streets in Fisherman's Wharf.

- The **Powell-Mason line** heads out from Powell and Market over Nob Hill through North Beach to Bay and Taylor at Fisherman's Wharf.

- The **California line** starts from California, Drumm, and Market in the Financial District and goes through Chinatown over Nob Hill to Van Ness Avenue.

Queues for the panoramic Fisherman's Wharf lines can be long, and the ride can be chilly when the fog rolls in. But many insist the experience cannot be missed. The California line is the least crowded but is considered not quite as scenic. Fares can be purchased onboard. All-day passes are available. Souvenir tickets are also available at the kiosks on Powell and Market or Hyde and Beach. When in Nob Hill, stop by the **Cable Car Museum** *(see page 49)*.

You'll also want to ride San Francisco's **streetcars**, which provide daily service, thanks to the preservation efforts of the Market Street Railway organization *(415-956-0472, www.streetcar.org)*. The cars run along Market and the Embarcadero to Fisherman's Wharf. Their historic trolleys include "Streamliner" Art Deco streetcars and vintage trams from Milan, Italy, dating back to the 1920s. The six-mile **F-Market & Wharves Historic Streetcar Line**, or **F-line**, starts at Harvey Milk Plaza at 17th, Castro, and Market streets, and culminates at Fisherman's Wharf. Plans are underway for an **E-line** to connect more than 20 key destinations along the waterfront. **Streetcars** accept MUNI passes and transfers. Learn more about their history at the **San Francisco Railway Museum** *(see page 79)*.

CITY TOURS:

Adventure Cat Sailing Charters offers exciting daytime and sunset Bay cruises on a 55- or 65-foot catamaran *(Pier 39, J-Dock, 415-777-1630, www.adventurecat.com)*

Hornblower Cruises pampers you aboard luxury yachts *(Pier 3, the Embarcadero, 888-467-6256, www. hornblower.com)*

SF Bay Whale Watching takes you to the Farallon Islands in search of gray, blue, or humpback whales *(415-331-6267, www.sfbaywhalewatching.com)*

GoCar Tours. See the sights in a bright yellow, two-passenger, GPS-guided "storytelling" car *(2715 Hyde St., Fisherman's Wharf; 321 Mason St., Union Sq.; 415-441-5695, www.gocarsf.com)*

Blazing Saddles offers self-guided "Bike the Bridge" tours. Or rent its MP3 player audio tour; it explains Golden Gate Bridge history and guides you to Sausalito in Marin County. Human guides available, too *(2715 Hyde St., 415-202-8888, www.blazingsaddles.com)*

Barbary Coast Trail. Bronze medallions and arrows embedded in the sidewalk point the way to 20 of the city's top historic sites along a 3.8-mile route. Group tours available *(415-454-2355, www.barbarycoasttrail.org)*

City Guides. Themed tours, including "Bawdy and Naughty," "Art Deco Marina," "Ghost

Walk at the Palace" *(San Francisco Public Library, Main Library, 100 Larkin St., 415-557-4266, www.sfcity guides.org)*

All About Chinatown Walking Tours. Visit a fortune cookie factory, Buddhist temple, herbal pharmacy, and more *(415-982-8839, www.allaboutchinatown.com)*

The Wok Wiz specializes in cooking classes, feasting tours, and Chinatown tours, including "I Can't Believe I Ate My Way Through Chinatown" *(650-355-9657, www.wokwiz.com)*

Local Tastes of the City focuses on filling, flavorful culinary tours emphasizing insider and specialty finds *(2179 12th Ave., 415-665-0480 or 888-358-8687, www.localtastesofthecitytours.com)*

HobNob Tours takes you through Nob Hill's mansions and Grace Cathedral. Breakfast, lunch, or high tea optional *(650-814-6303, www.hobnobtours.com)*

San Francisco Movie Tours. From *Bullitt* to *Vertigo*, visit the locations of your favorite movies *(877-258-2587 or 415-624-4949, www.sanfranciscomovietours.com)*

San Francisco Vampire Tour. Get acquainted with Nob Hill's Gothic side via this vampress-escorted tour *(650-279-1840, www.sfvampiretour.com)*

SEASONAL EVENTS

Winter-Spring:

Chinese New Year, February, with an illuminated parade and 200-foot Golden Dragon *(415-982-3071, www.chineseparade.com)*

Cherry Blossom Festival, April, Japantown, includes parade, taiko drumming, martial arts exhibitions, music and crafts *(415-563-2313)*

San Francisco International Film Festival, April–May, the longest running film festival in the Americas *(various venues, 415-561-5000, www.sfiff.org)*

Cinco de Mayo, Sunday closest to May 5, showcases Mexican American and Latin American culture *(Mission District, 415-206-0577, www.cincodemayosf.com)*

Bay to Breakers, third Sunday in May, 7.5-mile run with participants wearing costumes or nothing at all *(downtown to the ocean, 415-359-2800, www.baytobreakers.com)*

Carnaval, Memorial Day weekend, scantily-clad revelers celebrate Latin and Caribbean music and dance *(Mission District, 415-920-0125, www.carnavalsf.com)*

Summer:

Stern Grove Festival, June–August, series of Sunday concerts taking place in a natural amphitheater surrounded by eucalyptus, redwood, and fir trees *(19th Ave., 415-252-6252, www.sterngrove.org)*

Haight-Ashbury Street Fair, early June, arts, crafts, food, music, and more *(Haight-Ashbury, 415-863-3489, www.haightashburystreetfair.org)*

Union Street Festival, June, merchants, artisans, music, family activities *(Cow Hollow, Union St. bet. Gough and Steiner, 800-310-6563, www.unionstreetfestival.com)*

North Beach Festival, Father's Day weekend in June, celebrating Italian and Beat culture *(415-989-2220, www.northbeachfestival.com)*

San Francisco Lesbian/Gay/Bisexual/Transgender Pride Celebration and Parade, last Sunday in June, with costumes galore *(Market bet. the Embarcadero and 8th St., 415-864-3733, www.sfpride.org)*

San Francisco International LGBT (Lesbian, Gay, Bisexual, and Transgender) Film Festival, June *(415-703-8650, www.frameline.org/about/index.html)*

Fillmore Jazz Festival, weekend closest to July 4, West Coast's largest free jazz festival *(800-310-6563, www.fillmorejazzfestival. com)*

Cable Car Bell-Ringing Contest, July, cable crew members show their stuff *(Union Sq., 415-474-1887, www.cable carmuseum.org/ringers.html)*

Fall:

San Francisco Blues Festival, September *(Great Meadow near Ft. Mason, Marina, 415-979-5588, www.sfblues. com)*

Chinatown Autumn Moon Festival, September, lion dancers, taiko drummers, martial artists, and more *(Grant Ave., 415-982-6306, www.moonfestival.org)*

Folsom Street Fair, last Sunday in September, leather, whips, chains, and gender bending *(415-861-3247, www.folsomstreetfair.org)*

Halloween in the Castro, one of San Francisco's craziest nights *(www.halloweeninthecastro.com)*

San Francisco Jazz Festival, October–November *(various venues, 415-788-7353, www.sfjazz.org)*

SAN FRANCISCO'S TOP PICKS

TOP PICK!

San Francisco offers an abundance of one-of-a-kind attractions, neighborhoods, and experiences for visitors. Here are 12 of the top picks, not to be missed:

- ★ **Golden Gate Bridge** *(see page 131)*
- ★ **Golden Gate Park** *(see page 153)*
- ★ **Fisherman's Wharf** *(see page 23)*
- ★ **Alcatraz Island** *(see page 26)*
- ★ **Cable Cars and Streetcars** *(see page 12)*
- ★ **Victorian "Painted Ladies"** *(see page 103)*
- ★ **Lombard Street, "the crookedest street in the world"** *(see page 33)*
- ★ **The Haight** *(see page 171)*
- ★ **The Castro** *(see page 180)*
- ★ **Chinatown** *(see page 57)*
- ★ **North Beach** *(see page 37)*
- ★ **Coit Tower** *(see page 38)*

chapter 1

FISHERMAN'S WHARF

RUSSIAN HILL

NORTH BEACH

Places to See:

1. Port Walk
2. Boudin at the Wharf
3. Pier 39
4. Ghirardelli Square
5. The Cannery
   at Del Monte Square
6. San Francisco Maritime
   National Historical Park
7. USS *Pampanito*
8. SS *Jeremiah O'Brien*
9. ALCATRAZ ★
10. Angel Island
11. Musée Mécanique
12. Aquarium of the Bay
13. Ripley's Believe It or Not!
    Museum
14. Wax Museum
33. LOMBARD STREET ★
34. Macondray Lane
35. Ina Coolbrith Park
36. San Francisco Art Institute
56. Telegraph Hill
57. COIT TOWER ★
58. Filbert Street Steps
59. Washington Square
60. Sts. Peter and Paul Church

61. St. Francis of Assisi Church
62. City Lights Booksellers
    & Publishers
63. Beat Museum
64. North Beach Museum
65. Club Fugazi's Beach Blanket
    Babylon

Places to Eat & Drink:

15. Restaurant Gary Danko
16. Ana Mandara
17. A. Sabella's
18. Alioto's
19. Scoma's
20. Castagnola's
21. Forbes Island
22. Buena Vista Café
23. Lou's Pier 47
24. Fiddler's Green
37. La Folie
38. Luella
39. Yabbie's Coastal Kitchen
40. Frascati
41. Polkers
42. Pesce
43. Le Petit Robert
44. Swensen's Ice Cream

★ *Top Picks*

FISHERMAN'S WHARF

B: 10, 30, 47
Powell-Hyde cable car, Powell-Mason cable car,
F-line streetcar

• SNAPSHOT •

Welcome to San Francisco's tourist hub!
★**FISHERMAN'S WHARF** and the northern
waterfront, including the Pier 39 complex,
The Cannery, and Ghirardelli Square, draw millions of
visitors each year, more than any other area of the city.
Look beyond the souvenir stands and snack shacks;
you'll discover myriad attractions, specialty stores, and
destination restaurants. Tour historic ships, head out for
a day of fishing, or take a bay cruise. And don't miss the
boat to Alcatraz *(see page 26)*, considered one of San
Francisco's best day trips.

PLACES TO SEE
Landmarks:

Though the area referred to as
Fisherman's Wharf *(www.fishermans
wharf.org)* spans the northern waterfront, the Wharf itself runs along
Jefferson Street between Powell and
Hyde. Most activity takes place at **Pier
45** *(Jefferson and Taylor)*, the site of the

fishing fleet and seafood stands. Here in **Fish Alley**, fishermen bring in their catch in the wee hours of the morning, as they have for more than a century. Take a self-guided tour with **Port Walk (1)** *(from Ferry Arch to Hyde St. Pier, www.fishermanswharf.org)*; its 30 interpretive signs detail the area's history. Tempting bakery tours and a museum await at **Boudin at the Wharf (2)** *(160 Jefferson St., 415-928-1849, www.boudin bakery.com)*, makers of San Francisco's famed sourdough bread. Also on the waterfront: **Pier 39 (3)** *(Beach St. and the Embarcadero, 415-981-PIER, www.pier39.com)*, a bustling complex of shops, restaurants, and attractions. Don't miss the stars of the show—the bevy of sun-bathing sea lions at the pier's West Marina. They first appeared here after the 1989 Loma Prieta Earthquake; thanks to an ample herring supply and a protected environment, they now number into the hundreds. Marine Mammal Center volunteers are often around on weekends to offer informal information about the appealing creatures.

Historic **Ghirardelli Square (4)** *(900 N. Point St., 415-775-5500, www.ghirardellisq.com)*, another dining/shopping complex, is home to the city's famed Ghirardelli chocolate. Company founder, Italian-born Domenico Ghirardelli, established a San Francisco store in the mid-1800s. His sons later purchased an entire block and built the Chocolate and Cocoa Buildings, the Clock Tower, and the Power House. From 1907 to 1937, the buildings now housing **The Cannery at Del Monte Square (5)** *(2801 Leavenworth St., 415-771-3112, www.delmontesquare.com)* and the Argonaut Hotel (27) *(see page 31)*, served as the former Del Monte Plant Number 1, the world's largest peach cannery. Today, the square's European-style marketplace delights visitors with an olive tree-lined courtyard, cafés, and three levels of walkways and shops.

Waterfront attractions include the **San Francisco Maritime National Historical Park (6)** *(415-447-5000, www.nps.gov/safr)*. Its **Maritime Museum** *(900 Beach St.)* focuses on seafaring and the Gold Rush. Learn about the people who worked on the waterfront at the Visitor Center inside the Argonaut Hotel (27) *(see page 31)*. The national park also includes the **Hyde Street Pier** *(415-556-3002)*, an outdoor museum featuring historic small craft and landmark vessels. See the *Eureka* paddle steamboat, the schooner *C. A. Thayer*, and the Scottish square-rigger *Balclutha*, which co-starred with Charles Laughton and Clark Gable in the 1935 film *Mutiny on the Bounty*. The WWII submarine **USS *Pampanito* (7)** *(Pier 45, 415-561-6662, www.maritime.org/pamp home.htm)* is also part of the park. You'll find it next to Liberty Ship **SS *Jeremiah O'Brien* (8)** *(Pier 45, 415-544-0100, www.ssjeremiahobrien.org)*, one of 5,000 armada vessels that stormed Normandy on D-Day.

TOP PICK!

No trip to San Francisco is complete without a visit to ★**ALCATRAZ (9)** *(www.nps.gov/alcatraz)*, "The Rock." This former military prison and notorious maximum security federal penitentiary is now operated by the National Park Service. More than 1,545 men served time here, including Al Capone, George "Machine Gun" Kelly, Robert Stroud ("The Birdman of Alcatraz"), and Alvin "Creepy" Karpis, the last Public Enemy Number 1. The stark island was billed as a model facility for isolating "difficult" inmates. In truth, it cost a fortune to provide food and supplies for prisoners, correctional officers, and officers' families, who also resided here; it was closed in 1963. Today, visitors can tour the remains of the prison and cellhouse, including D-Block's grim solitary confinement cells and the siege-proof control room, and learn about famous escape attempts and life behind bars. The island's museum displays escape materials and artwork made by prisoners. An award-winning audio tour, featuring interviews with correctional officers and inmates, is included. You'll also learn about the American Indian takeover of the island from 1969 to 1971; though unsuccessful, the occupation launched the modern Native American movement. Rangers provide information about the island's tide pools, bird colonies (*Alcatraz* means "Pelican Island"), and other wildlife, too. Interpretive walks are offered. Note: terrain is rugged, and fog and wind can make it chilly. Wear comfortable shoes and dress in layers. Book ahead (especially in summer) through **Alcatraz Cruises** *(Pier 33, 415-981-ROCK, or 415-981-7625, www.alcatrazcruises.com)*.

Several ferry companies service **Angel Island (10)** *(415-435-3522, www.angelisland.org)*, which boasts great views from Mt. Livermore, the area's highest peak. The island also offers parkland and trails for bikers, hikers, campers, and picnickers. Or take a sunset bay cruise via **Red and White Fleet** *(415-673-2900, www.redandwhite. com)* or other ferry fleets. Fishing boats along Jefferson offer one-hour cruises and all-day fishing trips.

Arts & Entertainment:

Street performers frequent **Fisherman's Wharf**. Magicians, comedians, and mimes entertain **Pier 39 (3)** visitors daily at the Crystal Geyser Center Stage. The courtyards at **Ghirardelli Square (4)** and **The Cannery (5)** often offer live music. Don't miss **Musée Mécanique (11)** *(Pier 45, Shed A, 415-346-2000, www.musee mechanique.org)*, a collection of more than 300 antique arcade games, coin-operated pianos, and animated life-size figures. The collection shares space with **Amusing America** *(415-537-1105)*, a survey of amusement parks, arcades, and world's fairs. **Green Room Comedy Club** at **The Cannery (5)** *(2801 Leavenworth St., S. Bldg., Courtyard Level, 415-674-9333)* features top talent.

Kids:

Take them to the **Maritime National Historical Park (6)** *(see page 25)*. At **Pier 39 (3)**, they can ride a hand-painted carousel, bounce on the **Frequent Flyers** bungee trampoline *(415-981-6300)*, or enter a world of high-action film simulation at **Turbo Ride** *(415-392-8872)*. At **Aquarium of the Bay (12)** *(the Embarcadero at Beach, 888-SEA-DIVE)*, ride a moving walkway through a 300-foot, see-through tunnel; you'll be surrounded by bat rays, giant Pacific octopi, and other denizens of the deep. **Ripley's Believe It or Not! Museum (13)** *(175 Jefferson St., 415-771-6188, www.ripleysf.com, check Web site for coupons)* will impress with its two-headed calf, matchstick cable car, and other exhibits. San Francisco's **Wax Museum (14)** *(145 Jefferson St., 415-885-4834, www.waxmuseum.com, check Web site for discounts/offers before you go)*, one of the country's largest, includes wax celebrities, Chamber of Horrors, and King Tut's Tomb. Make your own teddy bear at the working **Basic Brown Bear Factory** at **The Cannery (5)** *(2801 Leavenworth St., S. Bldg., 2nd Level, 866-5BB-BEAR, www.basicbrown bear.com)*.

PLACES TO EAT & DRINK
Where to Eat:
The classic Wharf dining experience entails a takeaway bread bowl of creamy clam chowder, or fresh Dungeness crab (a Pacific-coast staple known for its sweet, tender meat) cracked to order, or crab cocktail from a seafood stall (you'll find benches by the fishing fleet docks). Exceptions include five-star **Restaurant Gary Danko (15) ($$$)** *(800 N. Point St., 415-749-2060, www.garydanko.com)*, the place to go if you want to impress.

The menu spotlights seasonal selections prepared in classic ways, from New Zealand snapper with fennel purée to Moroccan squab. Make reservations well in advance. Enjoy French-Vietnamese food in a spectacular colonial setting (and save room for the mango spring rolls) at **Ana Mandara (16) ($$-$$$)** *(891 Beach St. at Ghirardelli Sq., 415-771-6800, www.anamandara.com)*, "beautiful refuge." Don Johnson and Cheech Marin are part owners of this acclaimed restaurant. Always a hit for its seafood, **A. Sabella's (17) ($)** *(2766 Taylor St., 415-771-6775, www.asabellas.com)* was started by Sicilian immigrants in the 1920s. **Alioto's (18) ($$)** *(8 Fisherman's Wharf, Taylor at Jefferson, 415-673-0183, www.aliotos.com)* is an inviting family-run restaurant with tremendous views. **Scoma's (19) ($$-$$$)** *(Pier 47, 415-771-4383, www.scomas.com)* looks weathered from the outside, but is in fact one of the highest grossing seafood restaurants in the U.S.! Venerable **Castagnola's (20) ($$)** *(286 Jefferson St., 415-776-5015, www.castagnolasf.com)* has been pleasing patrons since 1916. Meet your inner Captain Nemo at **Forbes Island (21) ($$$)** *(Pier 39/Pier 41, 415-951-4900, www.forbes island.com)*, where you'll enjoy French cuisine in an underwater Tudor-style dining salon complete with fireplace and portholes from which to view passing fish. **Ghirardelli Square (4)** *(see page 24)* eateries include fresh-fish favorite **McCormick & Kuleto's ($$)** *(415-929-1730, www.mccormickandkuletos.com)* and **Ghirardelli Ice Cream and Chocolate Shop ($)** *(415-474-3938, www.ghirardelli.com)*.

Bars & Nightlife:

Warm up with Irish coffee at **Buena Vista Café (22)** *(2765 Hyde St., 415-474-5044, www.thebuena vista.com)*. The Wharf institution claims to have introduced the drink to the U.S.—now it serves as many as 2,000 a day! **Lou's Pier 47 (23)** *(300 Jefferson St., 415-771-LOUS, www.louspier47.com)* is a haven for blues musicians. Irish pub **Fiddler's Green (24)** *(1333 Columbus Ave., 415-441-9758, www.fiddlersgreensf.com)* features live music and barkeeps ready to pour stouts.

WHERE TO SHOP

Standout gift purveyors at **Pier 39 (3)** *(see page 24)* include **Crystal Shop** *(415-433-1272, www.crystal shopsf.com)*, offering paperweights, crystal Golden Gate Bridges, and Mary Frances purses. For Folkmanis marionettes, stop by **Puppets on the Pier** *(415-781-4435, www.puppetdream.com)*. **Cable Car Store** *(415-989-2040, www.cablecarstore.com)* has a nice selection of cable car mugs, toys, and more. Proceeds from sales at **Marine Mammal Center Store** *(415-289-7373, www.marinemammalcenter.org/contact/store.asp)* benefit Marin County's Marine Mammal Center, which rescues injured, sick, and orphaned mammals. **Ghirardelli Square (4)** *(see page 24)* merchants include **Wattle Creek Winery** *(415-359-1206, www.wattlecreek.com)*, offering tastings, and **Helpers Homes Bazaar** *(415-441-0779)* featuring new and vintage designer clothing and arts and crafts. At **The Cannery (5)** *(see page 25)*, see potters at work and browse creations of area artists at **Verdigris Clay Studio and Gallery** *(415-440-2898,* *www.verdigrisgallery.com)*. **Lark in the Morning Musique Shoppe** *(415-922-4277, www.larkinthemorning.com)* displays instruments from around the world. **Kachina Gallery** *(415-441-2636)* specializes in Native American jewelry, drums, and kachina dolls. If you're the paranoid type, pick up a bug detector at International Spy Shop (25) *(555 Beach St., 415-775-4779, www.international spyshop.com)*. It's all things Alcatraz at Cellblock 41 (26) *(Pier 41, 415-249-4666)*.

WHERE TO STAY

You'll find unique accommodations at Argonaut Hotel (27) ($$-$$$) *(495 Jefferson St., 415-563-0800, www.argonauthotel.com)*. Many rooms overlook San Francisco Bay; suites include spa tubs and brass telescopes. Best Western Tuscan Inn (28) ($$-$$$) *(425 N. Point St., 415-561-1100, www.tuscaninn.com)* features Italian décor. With free parking and a convenient location, Wharf Inn (29) ($$) *(2601 Mason St., 415-673-7411, www.wharfinn.com)* is an excellent value. Hyatt at Fisherman's Wharf (30) ($$) *(555 N. Point St., 415-563-1234, www.fishermanswharf.hyatt.com)* prides itself on plush bedding and top-floor city views. Marriott Fisherman's Wharf (31) ($$) *(1250 Columbus Ave., 415-775-7555, www.marriott.com)* is another option for comfort and location. Sheraton at Fisherman's Wharf (32) ($$$) *(2500 Mason St., 415-362-5500, www.sheratonatthewharf.com)* features Sweet Sleeper beds and a heated outdoor pool.

RUSSIAN HILL

B: 19, 45
Powell-Hyde cable car

• SNAPSHOT •

This largely residential area is quintessential San Francisco, with cable cars, chic boutiques, bistros, and secret stairways leading to some of the city's best hilltop views. Victorian houses peer out from tree-lined streets, while Russian Hill's main thoroughfares, Polk and Hyde streets, are home to as many dog grooming facilities as human spas and salons. Despite the perfectly coiffed pups and high-end dining, there is less pretension here than one would expect. The name "Russian Hill" comes from seven Cyrillic-inscribed gravestones found at the top of the hill in the 1800s. There has always been speculation as to who was buried here, but their identities remain unknown. According to one story, they were fur trappers; according to another, they were sailors from a Russian warship. The area was first settled in the 1850s by working-class families and in the late 19th century by artists. Current real estate prices draw more moneyed residents, but Russian Hill retains its Old World charm and is one of the city's best neighborhoods for walking and exploring. Its main claim to fame: Lombard Street, the zigzag stretch of pavement that attracts busloads of tourists every day.

PLACES TO SEE
Landmarks:

Whether viewed from the Powell-Hyde cable car, your automobile, or on foot, ★**LOMBARD STREET (33)** *(bet. Hyde and Leavenworth)*, is one of the most unique spots in the city. Though known as "the crookedest street in

the world," it is actually not even the most crooked in San Francisco *(see page 207)*. But the red brick–paved thoroughfare is far more photogenic, especially when the hundreds of hydrangeas surrounding the switchbacks are in bloom. The neighbor-

hood's mansions and upscale town houses make for a splendid backdrop. Its eight sharp turns were carved into Russian Hill in 1922 to aid residents in manipulating the 27-degree slope. If you drive, be aware that cars

enter on the Hyde side and that **Lombard Street (33)** only goes one way: down. Be prepared for bumper-to-bumper traffic and thrilling views (espe-

cially from the top) of Coit Tower, Fisherman's Wharf, Alcatraz, and San Francisco Bay. If you visit by cable car, you can get off at the top and walk down the stairs on either side. Russian Hill also enjoys literary fame. **Macondray Lane (34)** *(off Jones bet. Green and Union)* is the basis for Armistead Maupin's Barbary

Lane in *Tales of the City*. This charming, nearly hidden walkway is lined with lush plantings and offers stunning bay views. Another secret spot: **Vallejo Street Stairway** *(bet. Jones and Taylor)*; bordered by urban gardens, it lends picture-ready vistas. **Ina Coolbrith Park (35)** *(Vallejo bet. Mason and Taylor)* is a leafy hillside spot. Librarian Coolbrith, California's first poet laureate, was a friend of Samuel Clemens, Bret Harte, and Jack London. The 1857 **Feusier House** *(1067 Green St.)*, one of the city's famed Octagon Houses, is also worth a look.

Arts & Entertainment:

The **San Francisco Art Institute (36)** *(800 Chestnut St., 415-771-7020, www.sfai.edu)* remains one of the city's top art spaces. Aside from its student shows and relaxing courtyard, visitors are drawn by its two-story Diego Rivera mural, *The Making of a Fresco Showing the Building of a City*.

PLACES TO EAT & DRINK
Where to Eat:

Trendy **La Folie (37) ($$$)** *(2316 Polk St., 415-776-5577, www.lafolie.com)* consistently receives accolades for its French-Cal cuisine. At **Luella (38) ($$)** *(1896 Hyde St., 415-674-4343, www.luellasf.com)*, Chef Ben de Vries prepares nouveau, Mediterranean-influenced pairings in a hip lounge setting. **Yabbie's Coastal Kitchen (39) ($$)** *(2237 Polk St., 415-474-4088, www.yabbiesrestaurant.com)* serves up chilled seafood platters and heavier fare, such as king salmon with garlic mashed potatoes. **Frascati (40) ($$)** *(1901 Hyde St.,*

415-928-1406, www.frascatisf.com)
draws repeat customers for its russet
potato gnocchi and black-and-white
chocolate bread pudding. Weekend
brunch is the upper Polk experience.
Polkers (41) ($) _(2226 Polk St., 415-
885-1000)_ packs them in for everything from buck-
wheat pancakes to crab cakes Benedict. **Pesce (42) ($$-
$$$)** _(2227 Polk St., 415-928-8025)_ draws for its
seafood bar and Venetian _cicchetti_ ("chee-ketti") small
plates. **Le Petit Robert (43) ($$)** _(2300 Polk St., 415-
922-8100, www.lepetitrobert.com)_ offers everything
from steak tartare to apple- and brown sugar-stuffed
French toast. Treat the family at the original **Swensen's
Ice Cream (44) ($)** _(1999 Hyde St., 415-775-6818)_,
opened in 1948 by Earle Swensen.

Bars & Nightlife:

It's jazz for the older daytime crowd at **Cresta's 2211
Club (45)** _(2211 Polk St., 415-673-2211)_; at night,
patrons get younger and blues and rock take over.
Bacchus Wine & Sake Bar (46) _(1954 Hyde St., 415-928-
2633)_ features unique wines and sake cocktails.
Hungry? Order fresh _sashimi_ and hand rolls from near-
by **Sushi Groove ($$)** _(1916 Hyde St., 415-440-1905)_.
Locals pack **Tonic (47)** _(2360 Polk St., 415-771-5535,
www.tonic-bar.com)_ for drinks and Gummi bears
during the week; suburbanites pile in on weekends.
Sports fans frequent **Greens Sports Bar (48)** _(2239 Polk
St., 415-775-4287, www.greenssports.com)_, featuring
18 microbrews on tap.

WHERE TO SHOP

Packed into a few short blocks along Polk and surrounds, shops in Russian Hill tend to focus on home and gift items. Note: Many are closed on Monday. Swallowtail (49) *(2217 Polk St., 415-567-1555)* is a treasure trove of oldies and oddities. Jewelry is art at Velvet da Vinci (50) *(2015 Polk St., 415-441-0109, www.velvetdavinci.com)*, filled with one-of-a-kind sculp-

tural creations. Luxurious Martin Richards (51) *(1200 Union St., 415-885-5922)* offers everything from Anichini cashmere blankets to Diptyque candles. Upscale consignment boutique Cris (52) *(2056 Polk St., 415-474-1191)* carries both couture and street-smart styles. Molte Cose (53) *(2044 Polk St., 415-921-5374)*, Italian for "many things," offers antique and vintage-style jewelry and furnishings, plus new and vintage men's clothing. Sister store **Belle Cose** *(2036 Polk St., 415-474-3494)* offers women's apparel and lingerie.

WHERE TO STAY

Location and prices at the Broadway Manor Inn (54) ($) *(2201 Van Ness Ave., 800-727-6239, www.broadway manor.com)* are hard to beat. Castle Inn Motel (55) ($$) *(1565 Broadway, 415-441-1155, www.castleinnsf.com)* is basic, but friendly and convenient.

NORTH BEACH

B: 30, 45
39 to Coit Tower/Telegraph Hill
Powell-Mason cable car

● SNAPSHOT ●

TOP PICK!

Sandwiched between Fisherman's Wharf and Chinatown, ★**NORTH BEACH**, home of the Beat Generation, historic bars, and bookshops, is a slice of Europe in the U.S. Though land-locked today, the area takes its name from a beach that became a landfill during post–Gold Rush 1880s. Italian immigrants settled the neighborhood in the 1840s; by the early 1930s, five Italian-language newspapers were published here. In the 1950s, the Beat Generation embraced this then low-rent district. Its culture still reverberates around Jack Kerouac Alley, near Beat havens such as Vesuvio and City Lights Booksellers & Publishers. Joe DiMaggio also called the area home. **North Beach** keeps one foot firmly planted in the Old World with an *abbondanza* of family-owned restaurants, cafés, and pastry shops. Broadway remains the city's adult entertainment district, though the strip-club element has given way in recent years to trendy bars and restaurants.

PLACES TO SEE
Landmarks:

One of the **North Beach** area's biggest attractions is atop **Telegraph Hill (56)** in Pioneer Park: ★COIT TOWER (57) *(1 Telegraph Hill Blvd., 415-362-0808)*. The 210-foot white concrete tower was built in 1933 with funds bequeathed by the unconventional Lillie Hitchcock Coit, a wealthy widow known for her wit and way with guns and cards. Lillie grew up across from the city's Knickerbocker Engine Company No. 5 and became smitten with firemen. The "firebelle" wrote "#5"

TOP PICK!

beneath her signature and had it embroidered on her linens. Some say her tower is meant to resemble a fire nozzle. Take the elevator to the observation platform for 360-degree views. And take in the tower lobby's 1930s-era murals entitled *Aspects of Life in California, 1934,* offering detailed depictions of the time. More than two dozen local artists produced the frescoes; many studied under Mexico's famed muralist Diego Rivera, husband of Frida Kahlo. **Telegraph Hill (56)** itself was the site of a mid-1800s telegraph semaphore system that signaled the arrival of inbound ships. Today it's known for views and secluded stairways. The **Greenwich Street Stairs** link Sansome Street with **Coit Tower (57)**. The famous **Filbert Street Steps (58)** *(bet. Telegraph Hill Blvd. and Sansome St.)* are lined with gardens and Edwardian cottages.

Hear the squawking overhead? It's a flock of wild parrots—Peruvian Cherry-headed Conures—that makes Telegraph Hill its home.

A popular spot to attempt a tan when the fog clears is **Washington Square (59)** *(Columbus Ave., Filbert, Stockton, and Union Sts.)*, one of San Francisco's three original parks. **Sts. Peter and Paul (60)** *(666 Filbert St., 415-421-0809)* across the street was featured in Cecil B. DeMille's 1923 film *The Ten Commandments*. Joe DiMaggio's funeral was held here in 1999. Gothic **St. Francis of Assisi (61)** *(610 Vallejo St., 415-983-0405, www.shrinesf.org)* is now the National Shrine of St. Francis of Assisi. Visitors can view its murals and hear its 1926 Schoenstein pipe organ during free Sunday concerts. Film director Francis Ford Coppola restored the 100-year-old, copper-clad flatiron **Columbus Tower/Sentinel Building** *(916–920 Kearny St.)* in the early 1970s; it's now home to his American Zoetrope Studios and **Café Zoetrope ($-$$)**. **City Lights Booksellers & Publishers (62)** *(261 Columbus Ave., 415-362-8193, www.citylights.com)* was co-founded by Beat poet Lawrence Ferlinghetti (original publisher of Allen Ginsberg's *Howl*) in 1953. The store stocks poetry, Beat literature, and Left Coast books.

Arts & Entertainment:

Stop in at the **Beat Museum (63)** *(540 Broadway, 1-800-KER-OUAC, www.thebeatmuseum.org)*, and view literary ephemera, a rare

copy of *Howl*, even Kerouac bobbleheads. The **North Beach Museum (64)** *(2nd floor of the US Bank, 1435 Stockton St., 415-391-6210)* displays images and artifacts dating from 1850. Attracting everyone from tourists to Prince Charles and Lady Camilla, **Club Fugazi's Beach Blanket Babylon (65)** *(678 Green St., 415-421-4222, www.beachblanketbabylon.com)* musical satire skewers politics, social issues, and celebrities. Its spectacularly zany costumes are worth the admission alone.

PLACES TO EAT & DRINK
Where to Eat:

Italian-loving foodies flock to North Beach for its *ristorantes*. Here's just a sampling: **Fior d'Italia (66) ($$)** *(2237 Mason St., 415-986-1886, www.fior.com)* first opened in 1886 and claims to be America's oldest Italian restaurant. Singing waitstaff deliver hearty food and strong espresso at **Steps of Rome Caffe (67) ($)** *(348 Columbus Ave., 415-397-0435, www.stepsofrome.com)*. The place explodes when Italy's soccer team is on television. More sedate is **Steps of Rome Trattoria ($$)** *(362 Columbus Ave., 415-986-6480)*. It's a bit off the beaten path, but **Tommaso's Ristorante Italiano (68) ($)** *(1042 Kearny St., 415-398-9696, www.tommasosnorth beach.com)* is popular among locals and celebrities for its wood-oven pizzas. **Joe DiMaggio's Italian Chophouse (69) ($$)** *(601 Union St., 415-421-5633, www.joedimaggios restaurant.com)* is a new venture started by DiMaggio's granddaughters. The setting is 1940s supper club; the room is filled with Yankees mementos and photos of Joe and Marilyn Monroe. Non-Italian options include **The House (70) ($$)** *(1230 Grant Ave., 415-986-8612, www.thehse.com)*, acclaimed for Asian fusion. Locals line up for "m'omelettes" and sandwiches at **Mama's on Washington Square (71) ($)** *(1701 Stockton St., 415-362-6421)*. People watchers park at **Mario's Bohemian Cigar Store Café (72) ($)** *(566 Columbus Ave., 415-362-0536)* with a *focaccia* sandwich or a slice of ricotta cheesecake. **Washington Square Bar & Grill (73) ($$)** *(1707 Powell St., 415-982-8123, www.wsbg.citysearch.com)*, has hosted tourists and newsmakers for over 30 years. Famous **Caffe Trieste (74) ($)** *(601 Vallejo St., 415-392-6739, www.caffetrieste.com)* served Kerouac and Ginsberg, among other patrons. Some say Coppola scripted *The Godfather* here.

Bars & Nightlife:

North Beach is home to two top live venues: **Jazz at Pearl's (75)** *(256 Columbus Ave., 415-291-8255, www.jazzatpearls.com)*, with speakeasy ambience, and **Bimbo's 365 Club (76)** *(1025 Columbus Ave., 415-474-0365, www.bimbos365club.com)*, dating from 1931. The Beat goes on at **Vesuvio (77)** *(255 Columbus Ave., www.vesuvio.com)*. Jack Kerouac, Dylan Thomas, and other writers favored this hipster watering hole. The walls are filled with Beat memorabilia; signature drinks include the "Jack Kerouac" and "Bohemian Coffee." Bawdy Barbary Coast holdover **The Saloon (78)** *(1232 Grant Ave., 415-989-7666)* opened in 1861. **La Rocca's Corner Tavern (79)** *(957 Columbus Ave., 415-674-1266,* *laroccascorner.com)* opened a year after Prohibition; patrons have included Frank Sinatra and Joe DiMaggio. **Tosca Café (80)** *(242 Columbus Ave., 415-391-1244)*, another Beat spot, is known for its coffee liqueur drinks and vintage jukebox stocked with opera arias. You might spot a celebrity in the next booth. Divey **Spec's (81)** *(12 William Saroyan Pl., 415-421-4112)* has transmogrified from speakeasy to fisherman's club to Beat hangout to lesbian bar to oddball tourist stop. **Tony Niks Café (82)** *(1534 Stockton St., 415-693-0990)* serves fruity cock-tails in a swanky retro space. **Andrew Jaeger's House of Seafood & Jazz (83)** *(300 Columbus at Broadway, 415-781-8222, www.andrewjaeger.com)* offers New Orleans–style food and music; it's also the site of the historic Condor (in 1964, Condor diva Carol Doda became the nation's first topless nightclub dancer).

WHERE TO SHOP

More than a liquor store, Coit Liquor (84) *(585 Columbus Ave., 415-986-4036, www.coitliquor.com)*, owned by an award-winning winemaking couple, sells intriguing wines and offers daily tastings. Mixed Use (85) *(463 Union St., 415-956-1909, www.mixedusemodern.com)*, is what its name implies. Its top floor features vintage clothing, the bottom furniture and vintage electronics. With strong colors and bold styles from over 100 designers, Ooma (86) *(1422 Grant Ave., 415-627-6963, www.ooma.net)*, "Objects of My Affection," appeals to the sexy, feminine side. Trend-setting Macchiarini Creations (87) *(1453 Grant Ave., 415-982-2229, www.macreativedesign.com)* features everything from wedding rings to metal sculptures. Rosalie's New Looks (88) *(782 Columbus Ave., 415-397-6246)* has been renting and fitting fab up-do and bouffant wigs since 1957. Rosalie also sells vintage fashion pieces. A. Cavalli and Co. (89) *(1441 Stockton St., 415-421-4219)*, established in 1880, carries Italian books and

movies. Chocoholics must not miss XOX Truffles (90) *(754 Columbus Ave., 415-421-4814, www.xoxtruffles.com)*, renowned for its artisanal treats. Cool Japanese toys and collectibles await at Double Punch (91) *(1821 Powell St., 415-399-9785, www.doublepunch.com)*. Discover offbeat curios—old maps, wooden toys, and more—at Aria Antiques (92) *(1522 Grant Ave., 415-433-0219)*.

WHERE TO STAY

Hotel Bohème (93) ($$) *(444 Columbus Ave., 415-433-9111, www.hotelboheme.com)* has a 1950s Beat Generation look and feel. Antique-bedecked, value-priced Victorian San Remo Hotel (94) ($) *(2237 Mason St., 415-776-8688, www.sanremohotel.com)* offers comfortable rooms and shared baths. **Fior d'Italia (66)** restaurant *(see page 40)* occupies the ground level. Washington Square Inn (95) ($$) *(1660 Stockton St., 415-981-4220, www.wsisf.com)* offers European ambience and B&B accommodations with private baths.

chapter 2

NOB HILL
POLK GULCH
CHINATOWN
UNION SQUARE

Places to See:

Places to Eat & Drink:

Where to Shop:

Where to Stay:

"San Francisco itself is art,
above all literary art.
Every block is a short story,
every hill a novel...."

—*William Saroyan*

NOB HILL

B: 1, 2, 3, 27
California cable car, Powell-Hyde cable car,
Powell-Mason cable car

• SNAPSHOT •

Opulent hotels, upscale dining, and killer views all play into the Nob Hill equation. The hill itself tops out at California Street between Powell and Jones, where homes of the rich and famous once stood. Nob Hill "nobs" included the Central Pacific railroad's big four barons: Charles Crocker, Leland Stanford, Mark Hopkins, and C.P. Huntington; Gold Rush richies James Flood and James "Bonanza Jim" Fair; and the Tobin family, founders of Hibernia Bank. Most were victims of the catastrophic 1906 earthquake and fire that leveled the neighborhood. Rather than rebuild here, many moved to Pacific Heights. Upscale hotels and the Gothic Grace Cathedral were constructed on the sites of

the mansions. The Nob Hill area extends toward Union Square and the Tenderloin; called Lower Nob Hill, or "the TenderNob," it's filled with shops, restaurants, and neighborhood bars.

PLACES TO SEE
Landmarks:

Grace Cathedral (1) *(1100 California St., 415-749-6300, www.gracecathedral.org)*, overlooking Huntington Park, is the third largest Episcopal cathedral in the U.S. The doors of this soaring structure are casts of Ghiberti's *Gates of Paradise* from Florence, Italy's Duomo Baptistery. Its AIDS Interfaith Chapel features a *Life of Christ* altarpiece by artist Keith Haring. All are welcome to walk the cathedral's indoor and outdoor meditation labyrinths. **Huntington Park (2)** *(bet. Taylor and Cushman)* is the perfect place to rest after a Nob Hill hike. Its *Fountain of Tortoises* is a replica of *La Fontana delle Tartarughe* in Rome. Historic **James Flood Mansion (3)** *(1000 California St.)*, headquarters of the **Pacific-Union Club**, is not open to the public.

Kids:

See the inner workings of the world's last cable car system, including cables, brake mechanisms, and more, at the **Cable Car Museum (4)** *(1201 Mason St., 415-474-1887, www. cablecarmuseum.org)*.

PLACES TO EAT & DRINK
Where to Eat:

Fleur de Lys (5) ($$$) *(777 Sutter St., 415-673-7779, www.fleurdelysf.com)* sets the benchmark for sublime; former President Clinton invited Chef Hubert Keller to be a guest White House chef. Expect innovative seafood and Alsatian cuisine. The **Dining Room (6) ($$$)** *(Ritz-Carlton, 600 Stockton St., 415-773-6198, www.ritzcarlton.com)* takes fine dining to the max with plush décor and impeccable service. Tasting menus run three to nine courses. Don't forget the cheese cart. Savor the flavors of French Vietnam at **Le Colonial (7) ($$)** *(20 Cosmo Pl., 415-931-3600, www.lecolonialsf.com)*, a 1920s *Indochine*-style gem with rattan décor, ceiling fans, and images of old Saigon. **Brick (8) ($)** *(1085 Sutter St., 415-441-4232, www.brickrestaurant.com)* offers chic American fare. Enjoy a glass of wine at the copper-topped bar. **1550 Hyde Café & Wine Bar (9) ($$)** *(1550 Hyde St., 415-775-1550, www.1550hyde.com)* is known for organic Cal-Med cuisine and an award-winning wine list. Chef Dennis Leary's creative menu makes it worth the squeeze into 20-seat **Canteen (10) ($$)** *(817 Sutter St., 415-928-8870, www.canteensf.com)*.

Bars & Nightlife:

Nob Hill's hotel bars are the swankiest spots at which to sip cocktails. **Top of the Mark (11)** *(InterContinental Mark Hopkins Hotel, 1 Nob Hill, 999 California St., 415-616-6916, www.topofthemark.com)* stands out for

its "100 Martinis" menu and incredible views. **Tonga Room & Hurricane Bar (12)** *(Fairmont San Francisco, 950 Mason St., 415-772-5278, www.fairmont.com)* is a crowd-pleaser with faux thunderstorms and live "lagoon" entertainment. The happy hour buffet is a superb value. Posh **Empire Plush Room (13)** *(York Hotel, 940 Sutter St., 415-885-2800, www.yorkhotel.com/plushroom.htm)* hosts big-name cabaret acts. **Hidden Vine Wine Bar (14)** *(620 Post St., 415-674-3567, www.thehiddenvine.com)* serves select California and international vintages by the glass.

WHERE TO SHOP

Browse books on regional interest at **Argonaut Book Shop (15)** *(786 Sutter St., 415-474-9067, www.argonaut bookshop.com)*, the basis for Argosy Book Shop in Hitchcock's *Vertigo*.

Kayo Books (16) *(814 Post St., 415-749-0554, www.kayobooks.com)* is packed with vintage pulp. **Huf (17)** *(808 Sutter St., 415-614-9414, www.hufsf.com)*, from former pro skater Keith Hufnagel, outfits skaters and urban folk in cool

sneakers, hoodies, and more. Presentation is not key at **Asaka Fine Arts (18)** *(695 Sutter St., 415-775-5343)*. Look beyond the disarray and discover everything from 4th-century Afghan stone works to 16th-century Japanese Oribe dishes. **Australia Fair (19)** *(700 Sutter St., 415-441-5319, www.australiafair inc.com)* caters to tourists and Oz ex-pats with everything from Blundstone boots to boomerangs.

WHERE TO STAY

Nob Hill's historic hotels are attractions in themselves. InterContinental Mark Hopkins Hotel (20) ($$$) *(1 Nob Hill, 999 California St., 415-392-3434, www. markhopkins.net)*, a 1926 French Chateau/Spanish Renaissance landmark, has hosted everyone from Elvis to Elizabeth Taylor. Tony Bennett first sang "I Left My Heart in San Francisco" in the Venetian Room at Fairmont San Francisco (21) ($$$) *(950 Mason St., 415-772-5000, www.fairmont.com)*. You'll feel like a V.I.P. at Huntington Hotel (22) ($$$) *(1075 California St., 415-474-5400, www.huntingtonhotel.com)*, ranked among the world's greatest. Hitchcock filmed part of *Vertigo* at the York Hotel (23) ($$) *(940 Sutter St., 415-885-6800, www.yorkhotel.com)*. Enjoy evening wine tastings at Executive Hotel Vintage Court (24) ($$) *(650 Bush St., 415-392-4666, www.executivehotels.net)*, where rooms are named after Northern California vineyards. Celebrated French restaurant **Masa's ($$$)** is on the premises. Antique-filled Edwardian Nob Hill Inn (25) ($$) *(1000 Pine St., 415-673-6080, www.nob hillinn.com)* offers afternoon tea or sherry.

POLK GULCH

B: 19, 38, 47, 49

• SNAPSHOT •

A district in transition, Polk Gulch bridges seedier Tenderloin with upper-crusty Russian and Nob hills. Once an upscale shopping haunt and former gay center of San Francisco, the Gulch deteriorated in the 1970s, attracting drug dealers and the homeless. But new dance clubs and live music venues are changing the landscape, replacing watering holes of old, and wine bars and upscale eateries are now interspersed with old-school diners and discount stores. Though far from gentrified, the Gulch is becoming a real neighborhood and fast gaining popularity for its dining and nightlife.

PLACES TO SEE
Landmarks/Arts & Entertainment:

Venerable **Brownie's Hardware Store (26)** *(1563 Polk St., 415-673-8900)* has been an institution since 1905. The window is filled with photos of Polk in 1939, when it was decorated Old West–style to complement a local fair. Catch indie, foreign, and other flicks at independent **Lumiere Theatre (27)** *(1572 California St., 415-267-4893, www.landmarktheatres.com)*.

PLACES TO EAT & DRINK
Where to Eat:

Locals line up at **Swan Oyster Depot (28) ($)** *(1517 Polk St., 415-673-1101)*, renowned for juicy oysters. If there's a wait, Anchor Steam beer is at the ready. Treat yourself to something glazed from **Bob's Donut and Pastry Shop (29) ($)** *(1621 Polk St., 415-776-3141)*. It's open late enough for dessert or a post-cocktail guilty pleasure. Dine in a rail car from the area's old Key Line at **Grubstake (30) ($)** *(1525 Pine St., 415-673-8268, www.sfgrubstake.com)*. Elegant **Acquerello (31) ($$$)** *(1722 Sacramento St., 415-567-5432, www.acquerello. com)* brings fine Italian dining to the Gulch. At **Crustacean (32) ($$)** *(1475 Polk St., 415-776-2722)*, crab is served roasted, sweet-and-sour style, or drunken, soaked in wine. Your quest for lunch, brunch, or dinner may end at **O'Reilly's Holy Grail (33) ($$)** *(1233 Polk St., 415-928-1233, www.oreillysholygrail.com)*, filled with antiquities. Pop in for tea, sandwiches, and jazz at **Leland Tea Company (34) ($)** *(1416 Bush St., 415-346-4TEA, www.lelandtea.com)*.

Bars & Nightlife:

Trendy new clubs have opened along Polk, but a healthy amount of grit lingers on. **Hemlock Tavern (35)** *(1131 Polk St., 415-923-0923, www.hemlocktavern.com)* blends both, with a rock/punk jukebox and live music room. Gays, straights, and trannies mix at **Lush Lounge (36)** *(1092 Post St., 415-771-2022,* *www.thelushlounge.com*); expect odd drink concoctions in a dimly lit setting. **Red Devil Lounge (37)** *(1695 Polk St., 415-921-1695, www.reddevillounge.com)* is a venue for '80s revival acts like the English Beat and other live shows. Scenesters slurp mango margaritas and crowd the tiny dance floor at **Vertigo Bar (38)** *(1160 Polk St., 415-674-1278)*. Alluring French wine bar **Amélie (39)** *(1754 Polk St., 415-292-6976, www.ameliesf.com)* also offers late night, small-plates dining. Drink in the company of a nine-foot yeti at thoroughly tacky **Bigfoot Lodge (40)** *(1750 Polk St., 415-440-2355, www.bigfootlodge.com)*.

WHERE TO SHOP

Fields Book Store (41) *(1419 Polk St., 415-673-2027, www.fieldsbooks.com)* is filled with spiritual, metaphysical, and esoteric books. American Rag (42) *(1305 Van Ness Ave., 415-441-0537)* has clothing for everyone, including retro wear, trendy togs, and everything in between. Tiny

Venus Superstar (43) *(1112 Sutter St., 415-749-1978, www.venussuperstar.com)* offers edgy jewelry and clothing; shoppers find real gems here. Female-owned Good Vibrations (44) *(1620 Polk St., 415-345-0400, www.goodvibes.com)* offers a full array of sex toys and an antique vibrator museum. La Kasbah (45) *(1825 Polk St., 415-409-4866, www.lakasbah.net)* is filled with Moroccan home design imports and accessories, such as jewelry.

Cathedral Hill Hotel (46) ($$) *(1101 Van Ness Ave., 415-776-8200, www.cathedralhillhotel.com)* offers spacious guest rooms, a health club, and pool. Accommodations at Holiday Inn Golden Gateway Hotel (47) ($$) *(1500 Van Ness Ave., 415-441-4000, www.goldengatewayhotel.com)* lend views of the city.

"You wouldn't think such a place as San Francisco could exist...."

—*Dylan Thomas*

CHINATOWN

B: 1, 12, 9X, 30, and 45
California cable car, Powell-Hyde cable car,
Powell-Mason cable car

● SNAPSHOT ●

Foon ying—"welcome"—to ★**CHINATOWN**! This is America's oldest, established in the 1850s as a port of entry for Chinese immigrants, mostly men who came to work in Gold Rush mines or on the Transcontinental Railroad. It's also the second-largest U.S. Chinatown after New York. The vibrant enclave is two neighborhoods in one. Dragon's Gate leads to the tourist-thronged **Chinatown** on Grant Avenue, overflowing with antique stores, souvenir emporiums, and restaurants. The other, on Stockton, draws locals and mirrors the streets of Hong Kong, with fish markets, produce stands, and *dim sum* shops. The district's real flavor stretches beyond the two thoroughfares into side streets and alleys filled with herb shops, trading companies, and temples.

TOP PICK!

PLACES TO SEE
Landmarks:

Begin your journey at **Chinatown Gate (48)** *(Grant Ave. and Bush St.)*, or "Dragon's Gate." Made of materials donated by the

Republic of China (Taiwan), the gate is guarded by lion-statue sentinels. Bustling **Grant Avenue (49)** is the city's oldest street and the neighborhood's commercial heart. Fourth-floor **Tien Hou Temple (50)** *(125 Waverly Pl.)*, founded in 1852, is the oldest Chinese temple in the U.S. It's said Harry Truman's wife, Bess, received a prediction about his presidential election victory in a 1948 reading at Taoist **Kong Chow Temple (51)** *(855 Stockton St, 415-788-1339)*. A Bodhi tree on the rooftop of **Buddha's Universal Church (52)** *(720 Washington St., 415-982-6116)* is believed to have grown from a shoot of the tree under which Buddha reached enlightenment. **Old St. Mary's Cathedral (53)** *(660 California St., 415-288-3800, www.oldsaintmarys.org)* is California's first cathedral. The **Chinese Six Companies (54)** *(843 Stockton St.)* was founded in the 1880s by the Consolidated Chinese Benevolent Association to fight discrimination. **Portsmouth Square (55)** *(Washington, Kearny, and Clay Sts.)*, San Francisco's first plaza, dates from 1839. A replica of the **Goddess of Democracy** statue destroyed in the 1989 Tiananmen Square protests in China was placed here in 1999. The square is used by the community for morning *T'ai Chi*. The pagoda-esque bank at 743 Washington is the former Pacific Telephone and Telegraph Company and **Old Chinese Telephone Exchange (56)**. Operators had to speak five Chinese dialects, as well as English, to work here. The 1925 **Chinese Hospital (57)** *(845 Jackson St., 415-982-2400, www.chinesehospital-sf.org)* replaced a turn-of-the-century dispensary. Bruce Lee was born here. Explore a few of the neighborhood's famous alleys. **Ross Alley**, the oldest, once housed brothels and gambling venues; now it's the home of the **Golden Gate Fortune Cookie Factory (58)**. Pagoda Alley is **Hang Ah Alley** if you enter

from Clay Street. *Hang ah* means "fragrant." It was named for a perfumery once located here. **Waverly Place** was known as "15 Cents Street"—that was the price of a haircut by Chinese barbers.

Arts & Entertainment:

View photos, exhibits, and artifacts—from tong gang war weapons to a silver pagoda—at the **Chinese Historical Society of America (59)** *(965 Clay St., 415-391-1188, www.chsa.org)*.

Kids:

Watch cookies being made at the **Golden Gate Fortune Cookie Factory (58)** *(56 Ross Alley, 415-781-3956)*.

PLACES TO EAT AND DRINK
Where to Eat:

An old Beat hangout, **Sam Wo (60) ($)** *(813 Washington St., 415-982-0596)* is known for having rude wait staff ("No fortune cookies!"), especially infamous "world's worst waiter" Edsel Ford Fung, who died a while back. Today it still packs 'em in for basic Chinese fare. **House of Nanking (61) ($)** *(919 Kearny St., 415-421-1429)* is another institution; here, hour-long waits are not uncommon for pot stickers and green onion and

prawn pancakes. At **Jai Yun (62) ($$)** *(923 Pacific Ave., 415-981-7438)* Chef Chia-Ji Nei's Shanghai-style specials include quail soup and basil-mushroom stir fry. Locals love **Yuet Lee Chinese Seafood Restaurant (63) ($)** *(1300 Stockton St., 415-982-6020)*, especially after hours. Stop by at 2:00 AM for salt-and-pepper squid or frog legs. **Hunan Home's Restaurant (64) ($)** *(622 Jackson St, 415-982-2844)* is considered one of the city's best Hunan eateries. **Great Eastern (65) ($-$$)** *(649 Jackson St., 415-986-2500)* specializes in Cantonese fare, as does popular **R&G Lounge (66) ($-$$)** *(631 Kearny St., 415-982-7877, www.rnglounge.com)*. Satisfy your sweet tooth with an egg tart at **Golden Gate Bakery (67) ($)** *(1029 Grant Ave., 415-781-2627)*. Learn about tea at the tranquil **Imperial Tea Court (68) ($)** *(1411 Powell St., 415-788-6080, www.imperialtea.com)*. Try Imperial Silver Needle Jasmine or Organic Gunpowder.

Bars & Nightlife:

Li Po (69) *(916 Grant Ave., 415-982-0072)*, with a '70s-heavy jukebox, is the definition of dive bar. The red-lit couches in back are perfect for mai tai tripping. Another hole in the wall: **Buddha Lounge (70)** *(901 Grant Ave., 415-362-1792)*, where strong drinks are dispensed under the gaze of the Buddha behind the bar.

WHERE TO SHOP

Chinatown Kite Shop (71) *(717 Grant Ave., 415-989-5182, www.chinatownkite.com)* offers amazing kites and accessories, feng shui items, and more. The Wok Shop (72) *(718 Grant Ave., 415-989-3797, www.wokshop. com)* stocks hard-to-find cookware. Dragon House (73) *(455 Grant Ave., 415-781-2351)* carries authentic Chinese antiques. At Asian Image (74) *(800 Grant Ave., 415-398-2602)*, you'll find Thai silk shirts, origami sets, candles, and more. Han Palace Antique & Art Center (75) *(1201 Powell St., 415-788-5338)* is filled with jade items, as well as vases, tea sets, and more. Eastwind Books & Arts (76) *(1435 Stockton St., 415-772-5888, www.east windbooks.com)* offers one of the country's most extensive selections of Chinese-language and Chinese-subject books. Locals line up outside tiny Sam Bo Trading Co. (77) *(51 Ross Alley, 415-397-2998)* to purchase candles, incense, and Joss papers—paper goods to be burned in tribute to ancestors and gods. The cabinets lining Great China Herb Co. (78) *(857 Washington St., 415-982-2195)* date from 1922 and are filled with herbal remedies.

WHERE TO STAY

Grant Plaza Hotel (79) ($) *(465 Grant Ave., 415-434-3883, www.grantplaza.com)* is a popular no-frills hotel just inside Chinatown Gate. Accommodations at SW "Sam Wong" Hotel (80) ($$) *(615 Broadway, 415-362-2999, www.swhotel.com)* are accented with Asian art. Royal Pacific Motor Inn (81) ($) *(661 Broadway, 415-781-6661, www.royalpacific motorinn.com)* offers comfortable rooms at good prices.

UNION SQUARE

B: 2, 3, 6, 9, 9X, 30, 38, 45, 71
Powell-Mason cable car, Powell-Hyde cable car, F-line streetcar, Muni trains and BART to Powell St. Station

• SNAPSHOT •

Love to shop till you drop? You'll love Union Square, one of the biggest shopping districts in America. But shopping has nothing to do with the square's history— its name refers to pro-Union rallies held here at the time of the Civil War. The most cosmopolitan part of San Francisco, Union Square compresses major department stores and ultra-chic boutiques within a few blocks. It's also home to San Francisco's theatre district as well as top restaurants and historic hotels.

PLACES TO SEE
Landmarks:

Union Square (82), at the center of the shopping district, was designed as a public plaza by engineer Jasper O'Farrell in 1847. In 1903, President Theodore Roosevelt dedicated its **Victory Monument**, the Corinthian column in the center. Today, the square boasts a terraced performance stage, a café pavilion, and light sculptures. Watch gripmen turn cable cars

manually at the nearby **Cable Car Turntable (83)** *(Powell and Market Sts.).* This is one of the city's most-photographed spots. The **San Francisco Visitor**
Information Center *(900 Market St., Hallidie Plz., Lower Level, 415-391-2000, www.onlyinsanfrancisco.com),* is next door. **Lotta's Fountain (84)** *(Market, Kearny, and Geary Sts.)* was a gift to the city from "Lotta" Crabtree, a Gold Rush–era entertainer. Locals gather here at 5:12 AM every April 18th to commemorate the anniversary of the 1906 earthquake. **Maiden Lane**, lined with boutiques, was once Morton Street, a red-light, high-crime district during Barbary Coast days.

Arts & Entertainment:

Presenting Broadway shows and top-notch homegrown performances, San Francisco's theatre district includes award-winning **American Conservatory Theatre (85)** *(415 Geary St., 415-749-2ACT, www.act-sf.org),* in the former Geary Theater. The movie classic *All About Eve* was filmed at **Curran Theatre** *(445 Geary St., 415-512-7770).* Productions by African American playwrights are featured at **Lorraine Hansberry Theatre (86)** *(620 Sutter St., 415-474-8800, www.lorrainehansberrytheatre.com),* named after the author of *A Raisin in the Sun.* **Marines Memorial Theatre (87)** *(609 Sutter St., 415-771-6900, www.marinesmemorialtheatre.com)* was once home to national radio broadcasts featuring Jack Benny and Frank Sinatra. To buy discount day-of tickets, visit the **TIX Bay Area** glass pavilion *(Powell bet. Geary and Post*

Sts., www.theatrebayarea.org/tix/tix_booth.jsp). Changing exhibits at **San Francisco Museum of Craft and Design (88)** *(550 Sutter St., 415-773-0303, www.sfmcd.com)* highlight toy designs, wearable art, tools as art, and more. **Xanadu Gallery (89)** *(140 Maiden Ln., 415-392-9999, www.xanadugallery.us)* is housed in a Frank Lloyd Wright building where a Romanesque arch and Guggenheim-like ramp lead to arts and antiquities from around the world. Large galleries selling works by masters and contemporary artists include **Weinstein Gallery (90)** *(383 Geary St., 415-362-8151, and 253 Grant Ave., 415-397-6177, www.weinstein.com)* and **Martin Lawrence Galleries (91)** *(366 Geary St., 800-510-2450, www.martinlawrence.com)*. The **San Francisco Art Exchange (92)** *(458 Geary St., 415-441-8840, www.sfae.com)* sells pieces related to pop culture: stage, screen, music, and sports, including works by Alberto Vargas, Paul McCartney, and Ron Wood.

PLACES TO EAT & DRINK
Where to Eat:

Sleek **Bar Crudo (93) ($$)** *(603 Bush St., 415-956-0396, www.barcrudo.com)* adds a twist to the standard oyster bar with a variety of raw fish. **Farallon (94) ($$$)** *(450 Post St., 415-956-6969, www.farallonrestaurant.com)* wins kudos for coastal cuisine and undersea fantasy décor, complete with jellyfish chandeliers. At **Michael Mina (95) ($$$)** *(Westin St. Francis Hotel, 335 Powell St., 415-397-9222, www.michaelmina.net)*, good things come in threes—three-course prix fixe; trios of *sashimi*;

trios of desserts—except the wine list, with over 2,200 choices. **First Crush (96) ($$)** *(101 Cyril Magnin, 415-982-7874, www.firstcrush.com)* has gained a reputation for small plates and California wine flights. *Maltese Falcon* character Sam Spade ate lunch at **John's Grill (97) ($$-$$$)** *(63 Ellis St., 415-986-3274, www.johns grill.com)*, home to the city's Dashiell Hammett Society. Toast the fabled falcon with the Grill's signature "Bloody Brigid." Syrup-smothered Swedish pancakes await at **Sears Fine Food (98) ($)** *(439 Powell St., 415-986-0700, www.searsfinefood.com)*, a city institution. The ambience at **Colibrí Mexican Bistro (99) ($-$$)** *(438 Geary St., 415-440-2737, www.colibrimexicanbistro.com)* is early 1900s cantina. Its celebrated guacamole is prepared fresh tableside.

Bars & Nightlife:

Ruby Skye (100) *(420 Mason St., 415-693-0777, www.rubyskye.com)*, located in a sprawling Victorian playhouse, is one of the city's top dance clubs. **Harry Denton's Starlight Room (101)** *(Sir Francis Drake Hotel, 450 Powell St., 415-395-8595, www.harrydenton.com)*, draws beautiful people with plush booths, stunning views, and "Cable Car" cocktails. Stunning décor is the allure of the celebrated **Redwood Room (102)** *(Clift Hotel, 495 Geary St., 415-929-2372, www. clifthotel.com)*. Its oversized bar is said to be carved from a single 2,000-year-old redwood tree. Antique-filled **Irish Bank Pub (103)** *(10 Mark Ln., 415-788-7152, www.theirishbank.com)* exudes authentic charm. This is the place for St. Patrick's Day.

WHERE TO SHOP

This is mainstream shopping central with retailers like Tiffany, Cartier, Macy's, Neiman Marcus, Saks, Barney's, the city's own **Gump's**, and the **Levi Strauss** flagship store. Westfield San Francisco Centre (104) *(865 Market St., 415-512-6776, www.westfield.com/sanfrancisco)* merged the city's historic Emporium with San Francisco Centre; now with cornerstone **Bloomingdale's**, it's the third largest shopping area in the U.S. Local boutiques include Métier (105) *(355 Sutter St., 415-989-5395, www.metiersf.com)*, a label hound's delight, featuring designers like Rebecca Taylor and harder-to-find names like Mayle. Margaret O'Leary (106) *(1 Claude Ln., 415-391-1010, www.margaretoleary.com)* is known for specialty knits and top designers. Miss Sixty/Energie (107) *(45 Grant Ave., 415-362-9475, 415-362-9470)*, two stores in one, caters to shoppers with a nightclub vibe. Men browse the main floor; alterna-hip ladies shop upstairs. Wilkes Bashford (108) *(375 Sutter St., 415-986-4380, www.wilkesbashford.com)* offers moneyed male clientele suiting and casual dress. Ted Baker (109) *(80 Grant Ave., 415-391-1256, www.tedbaker.com)* speaks to the hip sector with silk shirts, dinner jackets, and accessories. Shreve & Co. (110) *(200 Post St., 415-421-2600, www.shreve.com)* opened during the Gold Rush in 1852; today it spotlights known and emerging watch and jewelry designers. De Vera (111) *(29 Maiden Ln., 415-788-0828, www.deveraobjects.com)* focuses on jewelry by owner Federico de Vera, plus Italian glass, antique decorative arts, and more. Big Pagoda (112) *(310 Sutter, 415-296-8881, www.bigpagoda.com)* carries antique Chinese furnishings and fresh interpretations of same. Try out Macs and iPods, visit the Genius Bar, or check e-mail at the streamlined, stainless steel Apple Store (113) *(1 Stockton St., 415-392-0202, www.apple.com/retail/sanfrancisco/)*. Lush (114) *(240 Powell St., 415-693-9633)* makes fun soaps in sea vegetable, banana moon, and other flavors. Murik (115) *(73 Geary St., 415-395-9200)* offers Euro-style clothing and some toys for kids to age 12.

WHERE TO STAY

Sir Francis Drake Hotel (116) ($$) *(450 Powell St., 415-392-7755, www.sirfrancisdrake.com)* impresses with its grand lobby, Beefeater-costumed doorman, and **Harry Denton's Starlight Room (101)**. Smaller historic guest rooms at the Westin St. Francis Hotel (117) ($$$) *(335 Powell St., 415-397-7000, www.westinstfrancis.com)* offer Old World ambience; newer tower rooms are larger. Clift Hotel (118) ($$$) *(495 Geary St., 415-775-4700, www.clifthotel.com)* is home of the famed **Redwood Room (102)**. Its surrealistic lobby and elegant interiors are the result of a sensational renovation by designer Philippe Starck for owner Ian Schrager of Studio 54 fame. Singles can stay in an incense-perfumed Zen Den at Hotel Triton (119) ($$) *(342 Grant Ave., 415-394-0500, www.hotel triton.com)*. Larger accommodations include the Jerry Garcia Suite. Tarot readings held nightly.

chapter 3

FINANCIAL DISTRICT

THE EMBARCADERO

SoMa/South Beach

FINANCIAL DISTRICT
THE EMBARCADERO
SoMa/SOUTH BEACH

Places to See:

1. Pacific Exchange
2. City Club
3. Transamerica Pyramid
4. Bank of America Center
5. Mechanics' Institute
6. Wells Fargo History Museum
7. Pacific Heritage Museum
8. Punch Line Comedy Club
28. Ferry Building
29. Rincon Park
30. Justin Herman Plaza
31. Rincon Center
32. San Francisco Railway Museum
33. Contemporary Jewish Museum
34. Teatro ZinZanni
47. San Francisco-Oakland Bay Bridge
48. Pacific Telephone Building
49. St. Patrick's Church
50. Yerba Buena Gardens
51. San Francisco Museum of Modern Art
52. Museum of Craft and Folk Art
53. Cartoon Art Museum
54. California Historical Society
55. Museum of the African Diaspora
56. Zeum
57. California Academy of Sciences

Places to Eat & Drink:

9. Frisson
10. Myth
11. Aqua
12. Medicine New-Shojin Eatstation
13. Tadich Grill
14. Kokkari Estiatorio
15. Rubicon
16. Plouf
17. Bubble Lounge
18. Pied Piper Bar
28. Ferry Building
31. Rincon Center
35. Piperade
36. Boulevard
37. Ozumo

"What I like best about
San Francisco is San Francisco."

—Frank Lloyd Wright

B: 1, 2, 3, 9X, 10
*California cable car, F-line streetcar, Muni trains and
BART to Montgomery St. Station*

• SNAPSHOT •

The shops, antique showrooms, and restaurants of today's sedate Financial District cloak its infamous role in San Francisco history. Over 150 years ago, after newspaperman Sam Brannan announced that gold had been discovered, the city's population exploded—from 1,000 in 1848 to 25,000 by 1850. Aside from would-be prospectors, the invasion included gamblers, prostitutes, murderers—every element of riffraff imaginable. Australian convicts converged on Pacific and Broadway; it was dubbed "Sydney Town" but quickly became "Barbary Coast" after North Africa's infamous pirate territory. Saloons, brothels, and opium dens packed the area. Hapless sailors were "shanghaied"—drugged and placed on undermanned ships headed for distant ports. Australians would attack a victim, shouting, "Huddle 'em!" (said to be the origin of our modern word *hoodlum*). And the corner of Jackson and Kearny was known as "Murderer's

Corner." The enactment of the 1914 Red Light Abatement Act, followed by a 1917 police blockade, effectively put an end to the Barbary Coast. The neighborhood deteriorated until the 1950s, when interior designers and furniture dealers moved in. During the go-go 1990s, rents skyrocketed and high-end antique dealers took over.

PLACES TO SEE
Landmarks:

The old **Pacific Exchange (1)** *(301 Pine St., 415-202-9700, www.cityclubsf.com)* building was once the Pacific Coast Stock Exchange. The two colossal granite statues outside are named *Agriculture* (feminine figures) and *Industry* (masculine figures). The adjacent **Stock Exchange Tower** is home of the Art Deco **City Club (2)** *(155 Sansome St., 415-362-2480, www.cityclubsf.com)*. Tour its art and furnishings—including its 10th-floor Diego Rivera mural, *Allegory of California*—the first Wednesday of each month through the Mexican Museum *(415-202-9700, www.mexicanmuseum.org)*. San Francisco's most recognizable skyscraper, the 48-story **Transamerica Pyramid (3)** *(600 Montgomery St., www.transamerica.com, not open to the public)* is owned by the Transamerica Insurance & Investment Group. If you enjoy panoramic views, consider dinner, Sunday brunch, or cocktails at the 52nd-floor **Carnelian Room (\$\$-\$\$\$)** *(415-433-7500, www.carnelianroom.com)* of the nearby **Bank of America Center (4)** *(555 California St.)*, used in the 1970s disaster flick *Towering Inferno*. **Mechanics' Institute (5)** *(57 Post St., 415-421-2258,* *www.chessclub.org*) is home to the country's oldest chess club, as well as a 150-year-old library *(415-393-0101)*. Both offer free tours. Also of interest: Ghirardelli Chocolate Factory was first located at **415 Jackson** from 1857 to 1894, and **732 Montgomery** was home of the  fabled literary publication *Golden Era*; contributors included Mark Twain, Bret Harte, and Ina Coolbrith *(see page 34)*.

Arts & Entertainment:

Wells Fargo History Museum (6) *(420 Montgomery St., 415-396-2619, www.wellsfargohistory.com/museums/sf museum.html)*, on the site where Henry Wells and William G. Fargo started their business in 1852, showcases a stagecoach, gold dust, and much more. **Pacific Heritage Museum (7)** *(608 Commercial St., 415-399-1124, pacificheritage.citysearch.com)* features exhibits on Pacific Rim arts and culture. Famous **Punch Line Comedy Club (8)** *(444 Battery St., 415-397-PLSF; www.punchlinecomedyclub.com)* helped launch the careers of Ellen DeGeneres, Chris Rock, and other stars.

PLACES TO EAT & DRINK
Where to Eat:

Patrons at hip supperclub **Frisson (9) ($$)** *(244 Jackson St., 415-956-3004, www.frissonsf.com)* bask in a red-amber glow while waiting for crushed-coriander Hawaiian butterfish or organic *coq au vin*. Note: Its former chef, Daniel Patterson, is creating a new buzz with his latest venture, **Coi ($$-$$$)** *(373 Broadway, 415-393-9000, www.coirestaurant.com)*. Cal-French cuisine and warm, contemporary environs romance patrons at **Myth (10) ($$)** *(470 Pacific Ave., 415-677-8986, www.mythsf.com)*. Desserts are divine. At **Aqua (11) ($$$)** *(252 California St., 415-956-9662, www.aqua-sf.com)*, Chef Laurent Manrique amazes, from his *hamachi* appetizers to Alaskan halibut with creamed parsley, amaranth, and lemon verbena/oyster vinaigrette to candied apricot. Feel restored at **Medicine New-Shojin Eatstation (12) ($-$$)** *(Crocker Galleria, 161 Sutter St.; 415-677-4405; www.medicinerestaurant.com)*, including organic, vegetarian hand rolls and hot dishes. Stop in for "contentment hour" *shochu* cocktails. While newer dining sensation **Perbacco ($$)** *(230 California St., 415-955-0663, www.perbaccosf.com)* draws crowds for its Italian fare,

next door former Gold Rush coffee stand **Tadich Grill (13) ($$)** *(240 California St., 415-391-1849)* is known for seafood. Sip a martini at its original mahogany bar, or summon waitstaff with doorbells from curtained booths. For *taverna* delights in an elegant setting, try **Kokkari Estiatorio (14)**

($$) *(200 Jackson St., 415-981-0983, www.kokkari.com)*, where classics like *moussaka* and *dolmathes* stand alongside ravioli stuffed with wild greens and feta cheese. Owners Robert DeNiro, Robin Williams, Francis Ford Coppola, and Drew Nieporent gave **Rubicon (15)** **($$$)** *(558 Sacramento St., 415-434-4100, www.sfrubicon.com)* its initial star power; now its award-winning wine list shines with over 1,700 selections. Belden Place, San Francisco's "French Quarter," is packed with eateries. **Plouf (16) ($$)** *(40 Belden Pl., 415-986-6491, www.ploufsf.com)*, one of the busiest, specializes in seafood starters. Its signature steamed mussels are done up with sherry/garlic, coconut broth, or other sauces.

Bars & Nightlife:

Swanky **Bubble Lounge (17)** *(714 Montgomery St., 415-434-4204, www. bubblelounge.com)* serves over 300 champagnes and sparkling wines. The highlight of sophisticated **Pied Piper Bar (18)** *(Palace Hotel, 2 New Montgomery St., 415-512-1111)* is its  Maxfield Parrish mural *The Pied Piper of Hamelin*.

WHERE TO SHOP

Crocker Galleria (19) *(50 Post St., 415-393-1501, www.shopatgalleria.com)* houses three levels of specialty shops, including Versace and Polo. On Jackson Square, **Antonio's Antiques (20)** *(701 Sansome St., 415-781-1737, www.antoniosantiques.com)* is famed for fabulous offerings; clients include Ralph Lauren and Oprah. **Sarah**

Stocking Antique Posters (21) (*368 Jackson St., 415-984-0700, www.sarahstocking.com*) is filled with vintage Belle Époque and Art Nouveau posters. Cable Car Clothiers (22) (*200 Bush St., 415-397-4740, www.cablecar clothiers.com*) specializes in British items for men: fly-fishing caps, classic bow ties, and more. William Stout Architectural Books (23) (*804 Montgomery St., 415-391-6757, www.stoutbooks.com*) is a must for designers and architects. Jeffrey's (24) (*685 Market St., 415-243-8697*) stocks toys and comics; it's a great place to search for hard-to-find collectibles.

WHERE TO STAY

Sumptuous, historic Palace Hotel (25) ($$$) (*2 New Montgomery St., 415-512-1111, www.sfpalace.com*) was the site of the 1945 banquet honoring the opening session of the United Nations. Luxurious Mandarin Oriental (26) ($$$) (*222 Sansome St., 415-276-9888, www.mandarinoriental.com*) delivers the highest hotel views in the city and more threads than you can count. Galleria Park Hotel (27) ($$) (*191 Sutter St., 415-781-3060, www.galleriapark.com*), next to Crocker Galleria (19), offers comfy rooms, a rooftop park, and complimentary wine in front of its Art Nouveau fireplace.

B: 1, 10, 12
California cable car, F-line streetcar
Muni trains and BART to Embarcadero Station

● **SNAPSHOT** ●

Joggers, cyclists, and tourists converge on the Embarcadero, the two-and-a-half-mile waterfront promenade from the base of Telegraph Hill to South Beach. Its big attraction: the Ferry Building, a recently remodeled survivor of the 1906 earthquake, now home to gourmet shops, upscale restaurants, and a lively farmer's market. It's also a functional terminal for ferries to Marin County, Vallejo, Oakland, and Alameda. North of the Ferry Building, Pier 7, the city's longest, offers postcard views. Historic F-line streetcars skirt the waterfront from Market to Fisherman's Wharf. It's hard to imagine that none of this existed until recently. For 50 years, the area withered in the shad-ow of the Embarcadero Freeway, two lanes of 70-foot high concrete from Folsom to Broadway. The free-way forced traffic to bypass the waterfront; piers were abandoned, cargo ships chose to dock in Oakland, and the area became an eyesore. But in 1989, a mere 15 seconds changed all that. The Loma Prieta Earthquake caused massive structural damage, and San Franciscans seized the opportunity to close the freeway for good.

PLACES TO SEE
Landmarks:

The 1898 **Ferry Building (28)** *(the Embarcadero at Market, 415-693-0996, www.ferrybuildingmarket place.com)* is the launching point for the city's ferry fleet. During the 1930s, more than 50 million people crossed the bay annually, making this the world's second busiest transportation terminal. Now it houses over 40 mostly food-centered shops, cafés, and restaurants. Public art

along the Embarcadero includes **four bronze whales** in the pavement near Pier 40 and *Cupid's Span*, a 60-foot bow-and-arrow sculpture by Claes Oldenburg and Coosje van Bruggen at **Rincon Park (29)** *(the Embarcadero bet. Howard and Harrison Sts.)*. At noon, Levi's Plaza Park *(1160 Battery St.)* fills with locals packing lunches. **Justin Herman Plaza (30)** *(Market and Embarcadero)* attracts suits, skateboarders, and visitors. Its angular concrete fountain was designed by French-Canadian sculptor François Vaillancourt. You'll find more shops and eateries in **Rincon Center (31)** *(101 Spear St., 415-243-0473)*, a former Post Office building also known for its historic murals depicting California history by Russian-born Anton Refregier.

Arts & Entertainment:

San Francisco Railway Museum (32) *(77 Steuart St., 415-974-1948, www.streetcar.org)* preserves the history of the city's vintage F-line streetcars. The **Contemporary Jewish Museum (33)** *(121 Steuart St., 415-344-8800, www.jmsf.org)* presents art and educational programs. A planned expansion and move will relocate it to Yerba Buena Gardens *(see page 83)*. It's "love, chaos, and dinner" at **Teatro ZinZanni (34)** **($$$)** *(Pier 29, 415-438-2668, www.zinzanni.org)*, a nightly dinner theater spectacle featuring variety/cabaret acts.

PLACES TO EAT & DRINK
Where to Eat:

The **Marketplace** at the **Ferry Building (28)** includes hotspots such as **Slanted Door ($$)** *(415-861-8032, www.slanteddoor.com)*. This sleek Vietnamese restaurant is inevitably full, so reserve ahead. Another: **Hog Island Oyster Co. ($-$$)** *(415-391-7117, www.hogisland oysters.com)*, serving juicy sweetwaters, Kumamotos, and other varieties. At **Rincon Center (31)**, **Yank Sing ($)** *(415-957-9300, www.yanksing.com)* is known for great dim sum. **Piperade (35) ($$)** *(1015 Battery St., 415-391-2555, www.piperade.com)* celebrates robust Basque flavor with entrées like sautéed calamari in ink sauce. **Boulevard (36)**  **($$$)** *(1 Mission St., 415-543-6084, www.boulevard restaurant.com)* pairs Belle Époque surroundings with a French-influenced American repertoire. Bring an

appetite to **Ozumo (37) ($$$)** *(161 Steuart St., 415-882-1333, www.ozumo.com)* for masterfully prepared sushi, *sashimi*, and tidbits from the *robata* grill. DJs spin in its trendy Sake Lounge. A tourist favorite and setting for multiple movies, **Fog City Diner (38) ($$)** *(1300 Battery St., 415-982-2000, www.fogcitydiner.com)* surprises with upscale offerings, including a raw bar and small plates.

Bars & Nightlife:

Young professionals jam **Gordon Biersch Brewery Restaurant (39)** *(2 Harrison St., 415-243-8246, www.gordonbiersch.com)* after five. Beer not your thing? Sip a specialty martini on the patio. **Pier 23 Café (40)** *(Pier 23, 415-362-5125, www.pier23cafe.com)* is a cool-vibe venue with views and live music. **Old Ship Saloon (41)** *(298 Pacific Ave., 415-788-2222, www.old shipsaloon.com)* dates from 1849 and was once home to a brothel and shanghaiing den. Today it's a congenial spot for happy-hour libations.

WHERE TO SHOP

Try the **Marketplace** at the **Ferry Building (28)** *(see page 78)* for shops like **Book Passage** *(415-835-1020, www.bookpassage.com)*, **Far West Fungi** *(415-989-9090, www.farwestfungi.com)*, and **Scharffen Berger Chocolate Maker** *(415-981-9150, www.scharffenberger.com)*. The five-block Embarcadero Center (42) *(bordered by Battery, Clay, Drumm, and Sacramento Sts., 415-772-0700, www.embarcaderocenter.com)*, or the "EC" complex, has interconnected shopping levels with retailers like Ann Taylor, Coach, and Williams-Sonoma.

WHERE TO STAY

The vast Hyatt Regency San Francisco (43) ($$-$$$) *(5 Embarcadero Ctr., 415-788-1234, www.sanfrancisco regency.hyatt.com)* is a city unto itself with 800 rooms. Guests who stay at stylish Harbor Court Hotel (44) ($$-$$$) *(165 Steuart St., 415-882-1300, www.harbor courthotel.com)* have use of the state-of-the-art Embarcadero YMCA. Hotel Griffon (45) ($$-$$$) *(155 Steuart St., 415-495-2100, www.hotelgriffon.com)* garners kudos for impeccable service and stately décor. Many rooms feature whitewashed brick walls, writing desks, and water views. Amenities at Hotel Vitale (46) ($$$) *(8 Mission St., 415-278-3700, www.hotel vitale.com)* include rooftop soaking tubs, a yoga studio, and suites with Bose iPod docking stations.

"Money lives in New York.
Power sits in Washington.
Freedom sips cappuccino in a
sidewalk café in San Francisco."

—*Joe Flower*

SoMa/South Beach

B: 9X, 10, 12, 14, 15, 27, 47
30 & 45 to Yerba Buena Gardens and south
All Muni trains to Market, N-Judah Muni train along
the Embarcadero to South Beach and AT&T Park

• SNAPSHOT •

Originally called "South of the Slot" for its location opposite the Market Street cable car track slot, SoMa, "south of Market," offers endless dining opportunities and is the hub of the city's club and arts scenes. In Gold Rush days, SoMa provided affordable housing for a burgeoning population. Industry took hold after the 1906 earthquake, and factories and warehouses popped up where homes once stood. In the 1990s, dot-com money revitalized the area, attracting restaurants, nightspots, art spaces, and a new ballpark. Still, SoMa may seem very industrial. For visitors, the bulk of its attractions are found in three areas: Yerba Buena Gardens, the 11th Street nightclub corridor, and South Beach. Yerba Buena Gardens, spanning two blocks, is home to urban gardens, museums, galleries, and eateries. The nightclub district, along 11th and on Folsom, is a cleaned-up version of its former 1970s self, when it was known for S&M clubs and communal

baths. The AIDS crisis prompted their close, and gay nightclubs, music venues, and dance clubs appeared in their wake. South Beach is a thriving waterfront conclave; you'll find some of the city's oldest structures in its South End Historic District. South Park, epicenter of the 1990s dot-com explosion, is still popular for its cafés, especially weekdays. But the biggest draw is **AT&T Park**, home of the **San Francisco Giants** *(www.sfgiants.com)*. Since its 2000 debut, the park's name has changed three times, but nothing deters from its appeal for ball fans and its breathtaking setting on San Francisco Bay.

PLACES TO SEE
Landmarks:

San Francisco-Oakland Bay Bridge (47) opened in 1936 and plays second fiddle to the Golden Gate, yet remains one of the world's largest bridges. The 1926 **Pacific Telephone Building (48)** *(140 New Montgomery St.)* was the city's tallest skyscraper for 30 years. Tiffany windows and noon concerts are highlights at **St. Patrick's Church (49)** *(756 Mission St., 415-421-3730, www.stpatrick sf.org)*, dating from 1851.

Arts & Entertainment:

SoMa's **Yerba Buena Gardens (50)** *(bounded by Mission, Folsom, 3rd, and 4th Sts., 415-820-3550, www.yerba buenagardens.com)* is a welcoming space filled with walkways, gardens, and public art. The complex includes a butterfly garden, the Martin Luther King, Jr. Memorial

Waterfall, and **Yerba Buena Center for the Arts**, presenting dance, theater, and music. The avant-garde exterior of the **San Francisco Museum of Modern Art (51)** *(151 3rd St., 415-357-4000, www.sfmoma.com)* grabs the eye; inside, catwalks overlook four floors of exhibits. The **Museum of Craft and Folk Art (52)** *(51 Yerba Buena Ln., 415-227-4888, www.mocfa.org)* presents works from around the world. The **Cartoon Art Museum (53)** *(655 Mission St., 415-227-8666, www.cartoonart.org)* opened in 1987 with an endowment from Charles M. Schulz. The **California Historical Society (54)** *(678 Mission St., 415-357-1848, www.californiahistorical society.org)* displays fine arts pieces and nearly half a million photos documenting California history. **Museum of the African Diaspora (55)** *(St. Regis Twr. Complex, 685 Mission St.; 415-358-7200; www.moadsf.org)* spotlights the African experience.

Kids:

Zeum (56) *(221 4th St., 415-820-3320, www.zeum.org)* offers hands-on multi-media programs like a Claymation studio, as well as an ice-skating rink and bowling alley. Daily penguin feedings and other activities draw families to **California Academy of Sciences (57)** *(875 Howard St., 415-321-8000, www.calacademy.org)*, temporarily set in SoMa while awaiting a new facility in Golden Gate Park.

PLACES TO EAT & DRINK
Where to Eat:

It may take longer to choose the wine than the meal at **bacar (58)** **($$$)** *(448 Brannan St., 415-904-4100, www.bacarsf.com)*, with more than 1,400 varieties in its dizzying three-story wine wall. **Fifth Floor (59)** **($$$)** *(Hotel Palomar, 12 4th St.,*  *415-348-1555, www.fifthfloorrestaurant.com)* features a French-Cal menu and sommelier Emily Wines' (real name) superb selection. **supperclub San Francisco (60)** **($$$)** *(657 Harrison St., 415-348-0900, www.supper club.com)* is an exercise in sensual overload. Start with a drink in glowing Le Bar Rouge, then recline on a bed and enjoy an unpredictable dining experience that might include a massage, face painting, or aerial dancers. **AsiaSF (61)** **($$)** *(201 9th St., 415-255-2742, www.asia sf.com)* takes "service with a smile" one step further with "gender illusionist" waitstaff who perform hourly atop the red runway bar. It's innovative Vietnamese fare at upscale **Bong Su Restaurant and Lounge (62)** **($$)** *(311 3rd St., 415-536-5800, www.bongsu.com)*. Craving Vietnamese but not up for the scene? **Tu Lan (63)** **($)** *(8 6th St., 415-626-0927)* is famed for hole-in-the-wall fast food on gnarly 6th Street (hey, Julia Child once ate here). Join the line for legendary cream puffs at **Beard Papa Sweets Café (64)** **($)** *(99 Yerba Buena Ln., 415-978-9972, www.beardpapasf.com)*. New England ambience and American fare keep **Town Hall (65)** **($$-$$$)** *(342 Howard St., 415-908-3900, www.townhallsf.com)*

85

packed. Its award-winning chefs are also at the helm of hip **Salt House ($$)** *(545 Mission St., 415-543-8900, www.salthousesf.com)*.

Bars & Nightlife:

SoMa's bars, clubs, and live music venues stay amped till the wee hours. **111 Minna Street Gallery (66)** *(111 Minna St., 415-974-1719, www.111minnagallery.com)*, the place for art openings and film screenings, attracts the *très* trendy. **Varnish Fine Art (67)** *(77 Natoma St., 415-222-6131, www.varnishfineart.com)* serves cocktails as it showcases contemporary art. If doors are closed for a private event, head to nearby **John Colins** *(90 Natoma St., 415-543-2277, www.johncolins.com)*. Able bartenders and cool DJs ramp the vibe at **Wish (68)** *(1539 Folsom St., 415-278-9474, www.wishsf.com)*. Serving suds since 1908, **Hotel Utah Saloon (69)** *(500 4th St., 415-546-6300, www.thehotelutahsaloon.com)* is a Barbary Coast throwback. Mammoth multipurpose **Mezzanine (70)** *(444 Jessie St., 415-625-8880, www.mezzaninesf.com)* showcases live and electronic music, plus art and fashion events. Partiers of all persuasions head to **EndUp (71)** *(401 6th St., 415-646-0999, www.theendup.com)* for heavy dancing. Boz Scaggs' **Slim's (72)** *(333 11th St., 415-255-0333, www.slims-sf.com)* hosts alternative and hard-edge acts with a robust sound system. **Club Six (73)** *(60 6th St., 415-863-1221, www.clubsix1.com)* attracts those seeking a club sans hipster scene. Despite seedy surrounds, some of the city's most innovative DJs spin here.

WHERE TO SHOP

SF MOMA MuseumStore (74) *(San Francisco Museum of Modern Art, 151 3rd St., 415-357-4000, www.sfmoma.org/museumstore)* carries art books, imaginative jewelry, and educational toys. Jeremy's (75) *(2 South Park, 415-882-4929, www.jeremys.com)* offers top fashions at deep discounts. Some are display pieces, some are returns, but deals can't be beat. International collectors and novice oenophiles alike swear by the selection and staff at K&L Wine Merchants (76) *(638 4th St., 415-896-1734, www.klwines.com)*.

WHERE TO STAY

St. Regis San Francisco (77) ($$$) *(125 3rd St., 415-284-4000, www.starwoodhotels.com)* provides top-tier luxury, plus stellar restaurant **Ame ($$$)** *(415-284-4040, www.amerestaurant.com)*, French for "soul." Artful Hotel Palomar (78) ($$$) *(12 4th St., 415-348-1111, www.hotelpalomar-sf.com)* has a René Magritte Suite, complete with bowler hat, green apples, and prints by the Belgian surrealist. W San Francisco (79) ($$$) *(181 3rd St., 415-777-5300, www.whotels.com)* offers ultra-lush "Wonderful Rooms" and "Extreme Wow Suites." Westin San Francisco Market Street (80) ($$-$$$) *(50 3rd St., 415-974-6400, www.starwoodhotels.com)* displays art by David Hockney and Roy Lichtenstein. The Pickwick (81) ($$) *(85 5th St., 415-421-7500, www.thepickwickhotel.com)* made an appearance in *noir* classic *The Maltese Falcon*.

chapter 4

CIVIC CENTER

TENDERLOIN

HAYES VALLEY

WESTERN ADDITION/JAPANTOWN

CIVIC CENTER
TENDERLOIN
HAYES VALLEY
WESTERN ADDITION/JAPANTOWN

Places to See:

1. City Hall
2. San Francisco
   Public Library
3. United Nations Plaza
4. War Memorial
   Opera House
5. Louise M. Davies
   Symphony Hall
6. Asian Art Museum
15. Glide Memorial Church
16. Little Saigon
17. Luggage Store
18. Great American Music Hall
19. The Warfield
34. Artists Alley
35. Octavia's Haze Gallery
36. Isotope
51. PAINTED LADIES ★
52. Bush Street-Cottage Row
    Historic District
53. Cathedral of St. Mary
    of the Assumption
54. Japan Center
55. St. John Coltrane Church
56. African American
    Art & Culture Complex
57. Kabuki Springs & Spa
58. Fillmore Heritage Center

Places to Eat & Drink:

7. Jardinière
8. Careme Room
9. Ananda Fuara
10. Trader Vic's
11. Rickshaw Stop
12. Soluna Café & Lounge
20. Dottie's True Blue Café
21. Millennium
22. Cortez Restaurant & Bar
23. Red Box Sushi
24. Saigon Sandwich
25. Shalimar
26. Bourbon & Branch
27. 222 Club
28. Ha-Ra Club
29. Mitchell Brothers
    O'Farrell Theater
37. Absinthe Brasserie & Bar
38. Sebo

★ *Top Picks*

Where to Shop:

Where to Stay:

CIVIC CENTER

B: 5, 19, 21, 47, 49
F-line streetcar, Muni trains and BART to
Civic Center Station

• SNAPSHOT •

Aesthetically beautiful, culturally significant, yet socially challenged, San Francisco's Civic Center exemplifies the triumphs and trials that define the city. Civic Center faces problems similar to those of its neighbor, Tenderloin, with regard to drug dealers, panhandlers, and the homeless. Yet visitors will find architectural masterpieces here: City Hall, the War Memorial Opera House, and the Louise M. Davies Symphony Hall. The War Memorial Veterans Building along Van Ness is home to the Herbst Theatre, the San Francisco Performing Arts Library and Museum, and the San Francisco Art Commission Gallery. All are part of the San Francisco War Memorial and Performing Arts Center *(www.sfwmpac.org)*. You'll also find the Asian Art Museum here; it houses one of the world's largest collections of Asian art.

PLACES TO SEE
Landmarks:

Topped by the world's fifth largest dome, San Francisco's Beaux Arts **City Hall (1)** *(1 Dr. Carlton B. Goodlett Pl., 415-554-4933, www.sfgov.org/site/cityhall_index.asp)* rises over 300 feet and spans two blocks. The city's first city hall was destroyed by the 1906 earthquake; architect Arthur Brown, Jr., who designed Coit Tower *(see page 38)*, built this version in 1915, basing it on St. Peter's Basilica in Rome. Inside, an impressive rotunda and grand staircase lead to the mayor's second-floor office. Joe DiMaggio and Marilyn Monroe were married here in 1954. The **San Francisco Public Library (2)** *(100 Larkin St., 415-557-4400, http://sfpl.lib.ca.us/)*

includes a five-story atrium with skylight and a rooftop terrace. Tours are offered the second Wednesday of each month at 2:30 PM. The pillars at the **United Nations Plaza (3)** *(bet. Hyde and Market Sts.)* are inscribed with the dates various countries were admitted into the UN; the plaza floor spells out the goals of the UN Charter, adopted on June 25, 1945, in the **War Memorial Opera House (4)**.

Arts & Entertainment:

The **San Francisco Opera**, North America's second largest, is housed at the **War Memorial Opera House (4)** *(301 Van Ness Ave., 415-864-3330, 415-861-4008, www.sfopera.com)*, built as a memorial to WWI soldiers. The **San Francisco Ballet Company** *(415-861-5600,* *www.sfballet.org)* also performs here; it's the country's oldest professional ballet company. The San Francisco Symphony is based in another grand space, the **Louise M. Davies Symphony Hall (5)** *(201 Van Ness Ave., 415-864-6000, www.sfsymphony.org)*. The symphony is renowned for experimentation and has performed with Metallica and Elvis Costello. Sculptor Henry Moore's *Large Four Piece Reclining Figure* lounges before the building. The **Asian Art Museum (6)** *(200 Larkin St., 415-581-3500, www.asianart.org)* showcases nearly 15,000 objects spanning 6,000 years, and includes a functioning, traditional tearoom.

PLACES TO EAT & DRINK
Where to Eat:
Jardinière (7) ($$$) *(300 Grove St., 415-861-5555, www.jardiniere.com)*, blends French inspiration with fresh California ingredients. Live music lends the finishing touch. Students of the California Culinary Academy strut their stuff at **Careme Room (8) ($$)** *(625 Polk St., 415-216-4329)*; watch them work through the kitchen windows. Vegetarians embrace **Ananda Fuara (9) ($)** *(1298 Market St., 415-621-1994, www.anandafuara.com)*, "Fountain of Delight," a Sri Chinmoy spiritual endeavor. **Trader Vic's (10) ($)** *(555 Golden Gate Ave., 415-775-6300, www.tradervics.com)* is famed for mai tais and Polynesian cuisine.

Bars & Nightlife:
Rickshaw Stop (11) *(155 Fell St., 415-861-2011, www.rickshawstop.com)* shakes Civic Center with underground and name DJs, live bands, and funky specialty nights, like "Nonstop Bhangra." Ambient lighting, DJs, live jazz, and fruity cocktails bring the bar crowd to **Soluna Café & Lounge (12)** *(272 McAllister St., 415-621-2200, www.solunasf.com)*, but it's worth coming for lunch or dinner.

WHERE TO SHOP
The Monday/Thursday/Friday **Antique and Artisan Market** *(www.sfanamkt.com)* at **United Nations Plaza (3)** is a great place to browse for arts, crafts, and collectibles.

WHERE TO STAY
The well-appointed Inn at the Opera (13) ($$) *(333 Fulton St., 415-863-8400, www.innattheopera.com)* has hosted such stars as Pavarotti and Baryshnikov. Comfy Renoir Hotel San Francisco (14) ($$) *(45 McAllister St., 415-626-5200, www.renoirhotel.com)* is housed in a landmark 1909 flatiron-style building.

TENDERLOIN

B: 19, 27, 31, 38
F-line streetcar, Muni trains and BART
to Civic Center Station

● SNAPSHOT ●

The Tenderloin, with its strip clubs and methadone clinics, resists gentrification. But lower rents here have allowed recent transformation, with a few trendy bars, ethnic restaurants, and shops moving in. It's also drawn immigrants from Vietnam, Laos, and Cambodia, and a strip on Larkin is officially known as "Little Saigon." The Tenderloin's struggles can be traced to its history. After the 1906 earthquake, hotels sprang up here to accommodate those who lost their homes. Over time, the hotels became low-income housing. Speakeasies flourished. Police who worked this tough 'hood were paid more and were able to buy better, tenderer cuts of meat, hence the name "Tenderloin." Today, the Tenderloin's character varies. The area closer to Lower Nob Hill—the "TenderNob" or "Tenderloin Heights"—includes high-end hotels and restaurants. But the closer you get to Market, the sketchier it gets. Use caution and take a cab at night.

PLACES TO SEE
Landmarks:

Though **Glide Memorial Church (15)** *(330 Ellis St., 415-674-6000, www.glide.org)* first opened in 1929, it was reborn in the 1960s when pastor Cecil Williams opened its doors to addicts, gays, the homeless, and marginalized. On Sundays, its world-famous 9:00 and 11:00 AM Glide Celebrations, with uplifting sermons and songs, attract locals, visitors, and celebrities. Come early to get a seat. The Tenderloin is also home to **Little Saigon (16)** *(bet. Eddy and O'Farrell)*, a two-block stretch along Larkin, filled with Vietnamese restaurants and shops.

Arts & Entertainment:

Luggage Store (17) *(1007 Market St., 415-255-5971, www.luggagestoregallery.org)* presents art exhibits, musical performances, and more at 1007 Market, its 509 Ellis Street Annex, and in Cohen Alley *(500 block of Ellis bet. Hyde and Leavenworth Sts.)*. **Great American Music Hall (18)** *(859 O'Farrell St., 415-885-0750,*

www.musichallsf.com) features an eclectic range of music, from smaller acts to names like Sleater-Kinney. **The Warfield (19)** *(982 Market St., 415-775-7722)* showcases top rock acts. This 1922 theater can hold just over 2,000; its acoustics are excellent.

PLACES TO EAT & DRINK
Where to Eat:

Dottie's True Blue Café (20) ($) *(522 Jones St., 415-885-2767)*, a Tenderloin mainstay, is beloved for its breakfast classics: French toast, pancakes, eggs, and bacon.

Millennium (21) ($$) *(580 Geary St., 415-345-3900, www.millenniumrestaurant.com)* serves high-end vegetarian fare even carnivores love. **Cortez Restaurant & Bar (22) ($$)** *(550 Geary St., 415-292-6360, www.cortezrestaurant.com)* specializes in Mediterranean-inspired small plates, such as katafi-crusted crab cake with citrus-marinated cabbage and tarragon *aioli*. One of the 'Loin's hipper eateries, **Red Box Sushi (23) ($$)** *(581 Eddy St., 415-563-7888)* is famous for fried fire-cracker rolls. Larkin is lined with Vietnamese street food shops and restaurants. **Saigon Sandwich (24) ($)** *(560 Larkin St., 415-474-5698)* is hard to beat for inexpensive, filling *bánh mì*. The French bread sandwiches come with meats or tofu and are piled high with veggies. The Tenderloin is also called "Tandoorloin" for its Indian and Pakistani eateries, like **Shalimar (25) ($)** *(532 Jones St., 415-928-0333, www.shalimarsf.com)*, one of the first of such fast-food spots in the area.

Bars & Nightlife:

Owners of cool nightspot **Swig** *(561 Geary St., 415-931-7292, www.swigbar.com)*, have opened **Bourbon & Branch (26)** *(501 Jones St., 415-673-1921, www.bourbonandbranch.com)*, a reservation-and-password-only bar around the corner. Evoking a 1920s-era speakeasy, it emphasizes cocktails mixed with hand-selected spirits and homemade juices—no cosmos here. Though set in a sketchy location, **222 Club (27)** *(222 Hyde St., 415-440-0222)* is a hot underground spot. Head upstairs for strong cocktails and pizzas or downstairs for DJs and live music. **Ha-Ra Club (28)** *(875 Geary St., 415-673-3148)* is a landmark dive bar, with curmudgeonly bartender Carl pouring for regulars, and a few trendies popping in from Nob Hill. Notorious adult entertainment venue **Mitchell Brothers O'Farrell Theatre (29)** *(895 O'Farrell St., 415-776-1016, www.ofarrell.com)* offers live sex shows daily.

WHERE TO SHOP

The selection of small-production, hard-to-find labels at Napa Valley Winery Exchange (30) *(415 Taylor St., 415-771-2887, www.nvwe.com)* appeals to enthusiasts and novices alike.

WHERE TO STAY

Stylish Hotel Monaco (31) ($$$) *(501 Geary St., 415-292-0100, www.monaco-sf.com)* brings four-star glamour to the 'Loin; relax in its Roman bath–style spa. Opal San Francisco (32) ($$) *(1050 Van Ness Ave., 415-673-4711, www.theopalsf.com)*, a former speakeasy, offers comfort, charm, and value. Party on at the fabled Phoenix (33) ($–$$) *(601 Eddy St., 415-776-1380, www.thephoenix hotel. com)*; it's hosted everyone from Nirvana to Keanu Reeves. Try an exotic cocktail at its **Bambuddha Lounge**.

HAYES VALLEY

B: 5, 21, 47, 49

• SNAPSHOT •

It seems in San Francisco that when a freeway is torn down, a neighborhood springs up. Hayes Valley, once known for its drug dealers and dilapidated tenements, was reborn after the Central Freeway was demolished following the 1989 Loma Prieta Earthquake. Now it's one of the city's trendiest enclaves. The area gained notoriety when director Erich von Stroheim filmed his 1924 film classic, *Greed*, on the corner of Hayes and Laguna. Today, Hayes Valley is filled with funky boutiques, galleries, hip restaurants, and low-key bars that attract locals as well as Civic Center theatergoers.

PLACES TO SEE
Arts & Entertainment:

Fine arts gallery **Artists Alley (34)** *(345 Gough St., 415-522-2440, www.theartistsalley.com)* spotlights area artists, painters, photographers, and sculptors. **Octavia's Haze Gallery (35)** *(498 Hayes St., 415-255-6818, www.octaviashaze.com)* specializes in glassworks from Bay Area and Italian artists. **Isotope (36)** *(326 Fell*

St., 415-621-6543, www.isotopecomics.com) combines comic store, art gallery, and laid back lounge.

PLACES TO EAT & DRINK
Where to Eat:
Enticing **Absinthe Brasserie & Bar (37) ($$)** *(398 Hayes St., 415-551-1590, www.absinthe.com)* charms with its Belle Époque setting. Fish lovers will embrace **Sebo (38) ($$)** *(517 Hayes St., 415-864-2122)*, featuring high-grade cuts in its *nigiri* and *sashimi*. The impressive sake list at this sleek spot comes courtesy of Beau Timken, who owns True Sake (49) *(next page)*. Fanatical about its artisanal, micro-roasted beans, **Blue Bottle Coffee Company (39) ($)** *(315 Linden St., 510-653-3394, www.bluebottlecoffee.net)* does a brisk business from its tiny kiosk. Its specialty: aromatic slow-drip coffee worth the wait.

Bars & Nightlife:
Über-hip **Jade Bar (40)** *(650 Gough St., 415-869-1900, www.jadebar.com)* packs out, especially for happy hour. Décor includes a waterfall, koi pond, and one-way men's room mirror. Chill out with a mojito martini and downtempo beats at **Sugar Lounge (41)** *(377 Hayes St., 415-255-7144, www.sugarloungesf.com)*. Happy hours are known for quality munchies and a cool vibe.

WHERE TO SHOP
Ver Unica (42) *(437B Hayes St., 415-431-0688, www.ver-unica.com/vu)* spotlights vintage clothing and accessories from the early 1900s to the 1980s. Some pieces have never been worn; all are in exquisite shape. Need a corset

custom-fit for fetish, fantasy, or wedding? Step into Dark Garden (43) *(321 Linden St., 415-431-7684, www.darkgarden.com)*. Find fashions by independent area designers at RAG "Residents Apparel Gallery" (44) *(541 Octavia St., 415-621-7718, www.ragsf.com)*. Jet-setters and others find Flight 001 (45) *(525 Hayes St., 415-487-1001, www.flight001.com)* a great spot to browse for travel merchandise, both whimsical and practical. It's named after the famous Pan Am "Flight One," which began in San Francisco and bounced around the planet before landing in New York. Azalea (46) *(411 Hayes St., 415-861-9888, www.azaleasf.com)* owners Catherine Chow and Corina Nurimba feature private-label clothes as well as handpicked items by top designers. Men's and women's offerings include plenty of denim. Their in-store **Z Beauty Lounge** supplies hand and foot pampering. Accessories are a passion at Jacqueline Talbot (47) *(451 Hayes St., 415-643-1343, www.jacquelinetalbot.com)*; choose from one-of-a-kind hats, bags, belts, and jewelry. African Outlet (48) *(524 Octavia St., 415-864-3576, www.theafricanoutlet.net)* offers a kaleidoscopic array of fabrics, sculptures, and more. You'll find the largest selection of sake outside Japan at True Sake (49) *(560 Hayes St. 415-355-9555, www.truesake.com)*.

WHERE TO STAY

Homey Hayes Valley Inn (50) ($) *(417 Gough St., 415-431-9131, www.hayesvalleyinn.com)* offers European touches and common bath facilities.

WESTERN ADDITION/JAPANTOWN

B: 2, 3, 5, 22, 24, 31, 38

• SNAPSHOT •

Not long ago, the Western Addition was one of the city's most crime-ridden areas. Change has been slow, but this emerging dining/nightlife hub continues its recovery. Gold prospectors first occupied the area known then as the Fillmore District; by the turn of the century, it was home to a strong Jewish community and the city's major shopping area. The district survived the 1906 earthquake, and its residents took in much of the city's upended population, turning basements and attics into apartments. An influx of Japanese moved in, but their population diminished when they were forcibly moved to internment camps following Pearl Harbor's bombing. African Americans took their place, and the Fillmore became the "Harlem of the West," with world-class jazz and blues clubs, new restaurants, and churches. But two decades later the area was declared a slum; renewal efforts consisted of demolishing lovely Victorians and replacing them with drab housing projects. The Fillmore was renamed "Western Addition." At the same time, Japanese began to reclaim the northern part of the district, now Japantown. Currently, the area is undergoing a rebirth with the opening of the Fillmore Heritage Center.

PLACES TO SEE
Landmarks:

Though you'll find Victorian homes throughout the city, the most famous are located here along "Postcard Row." The **★PAINTED LADIES (51)** *(700 block of Steiner St.)*—Queen Annes turned out in hues of pastel—perch on a slope across from **Alamo Square**. Built in 1895 by Matthew Kavanaugh, the "Six Sisters" survived the devastating 1906 earthquake. They are now private residences. Afternoon is the best time for picture-taking; the sun illuminates the Ladies'

facades as well as the downtown skyline, which serves as a spectacular backdrop. You should be able to see the Transamerica Pyramid and dome of City Hall from the top of Alamo Square Park, which attracts families, dogs and their owners, and busloads of tourists. (At its center, near the top of the hill, you'll come across one of the city's quirkiest attractions: a **shoe garden**. The park's gardener began collecting discarded shoes—from ski boots to Cinderella slippers—nailed them to logs, and used them to plant flowers.) You'll find more historic homes in the nearby **Bush Street-Cottage Row Historic District (52)** *(Bush St., Cottage Row, Sutter St.)*. For contrast, take in the ultramodern **Cathedral of St. Mary of the Assumption (53)** *(1111 Gough St., 415-567-2020, www.stmary cathedralsf.org)*, said to resemble a washing machine agitator. **Japantown** *(www.sfjapantown.org)*, also known

as *Nihonmachi*, "J-Town," and "Little Osaka," is one of the few in the U.S. Its heart is **Japan Center (54)** *(Post and Buchanan Sts.)*, a complex of hotels, shops, and sushi bars, including Miyako Mall and the Kintetsu Building, joined by Peace Plaza and its five-tiered Peace Pagoda, a symbol of goodwill given to San Francisco from the people of Osaka. **St. John Coltrane Church (55)** *(1286 Fillmore St., 415-673-7144, www.coltranechurch.org)*, or Church of Coltrane, was established after the jazz saxophonist's death in 1967. Coltrane believed in the mystical power of music; the church's powerful Sunday noon Divine Liturgy jam sessions attract as many music fans as churchgoers.

Arts & Entertainment:

The **African American Art & Culture Complex (56)** *(762 Fulton St., Ste. 300, 415-922-2049, www.aaa cc.org)* presents art, drama, dance, concerts, and films. Enjoy its vibrant east wall mural, *A Celebration of African and African American Artists*. Unwind in the communal baths of **Kabuki Springs & Spa (57)** *(1750 Geary Blvd., 415-922-6000, www.kabukisprings.com)*. Tuesdays are coed; otherwise, women and men are admitted on separate days. The area's new **Fillmore Heritage Center (58)** *(1300 Fillmore St., 415-346-8880, www.fillmoreheritage.com)* includes a jazz museum, restaurants, and **Yoshi's Jazz House & Japanese Restaurant ($$)** *(www.yoshis.com)*.

PLACES TO EAT & DRINK
Where to Eat:
Powell's Place (59) ($) *(1521 Eddy St., 415-409-1388, http://powellsplace.citysearch.com)*, started by gospel radio personality Emmit Powell, features Southern soul food. Think fried chicken, corn bread, and sweet potato pie. Busy, funky **Nopa (60) ($$)** *(560 Divisadero St., 415-864-8643, www.nopasf.com)*, "North of Panhandle," imbues rustic, wood-fired cuisine with Cal-Med flavors. Ethiopian food and *t'ej* (honey wine) or Harar beer keeps **Club Waziema (61) ($)** *(543 Divisadero St., 415-346-6641, www.clubwaziema.com)* on the short list of the area's coolest digs. In Japantown, a loyal following frequents **Maki (62) ($$)** *(1825 Post St., 415-921-5215)* for its *wappa-meshi* dinners—meat or fish steamed with rice in a bamboo basket. Reserve ahead to embrace authentic sushi at tiny, 12-seat **Kiss Seafood (63) ($$)** *(1700 Laguna St., 415-474-2866)*. Crowd-pleasing **Little Star Pizza (64) ($)** *(846 Divisadero St., 415-441-1118, www.littlestarpizza.com)* is known for deep dish pies stuffed with fillings.

Bars & Nightlife:
At the apex of the sixties scene, the **Fillmore Auditorium (65)** *(1805 Geary Blvd., 415-346-6000)* played host to everyone from Janis Joplin to Jefferson Airplane. Today's lineup consists of top acts in varying genres. **The Independent (66)** *(628 Divisadero St., 415-771-1421, www.independentsf.com)* presents everything from indie rock to jazz. The spirit of the Fillmore District lives on at John Lee Hooker's **Boom Boom Room (67)** *(1601*

Fillmore St., 415-673-8000, www.boomboomblues.com), spotlighting blues and jazz. Rare and premium sakes make up the menu at trendy **Tsunami Sushi & Saké Bar (68)** *(1306 Fulton St., 415-567-7664, www.tsunami-sf.com)*. For champagne cocktails, try sister spot **Bar 821** *(821 Divisadero St., 415-596-3986, www.bar821.com)*. Exotic teas are featured at refreshing **Poleng Lounge (69)** *(1751 Fulton St., 415-441-1710, www.poleng lounge.com)*. Boutique-brewed sake, soju, and alcoholic tea elixirs are also available. Sip while nibbling from Asian small plates.

WHERE TO SHOP

You'll find silk-embroidered kimonos from the fifties and sixties and handmade *haoris* (short, kimono-style jackets) at Shige Nishiguchi Kimonos (70) *(1730 Geary Blvd., 415-346-5567)*. Designer Mariko Sawada sells *dupioni* silk evening coats and more at Sakura Sakura (71) *(1737 Post St., #363, Kintetsu Mall, 415-922-9744)*.  Narumi (72) *(1902 Fillmore St., 415-346-8629, www.narumiantiques.com)* specializes in Japanese antiques, especially dolls. Marcus Book Store (73) *(1712 Fillmore St., 415-346-4222)* focuses on works by and about African Americans. Kinokuniya Bookstore (74) *(1581 Webster St., 415-567-7625, www.kinokuniya.com)* carries Japanese *manga*, magazines, and Asia-centric books. Thanks to adidas and designer Yohji Yamamoto, the planet's biggest collection of Y-3 apparel is at Harput's

Market (75) *(1525 Fillmore St., 415-922-9644, www.harputsmarket.com)*; it also carries luxury fragrances and vintage and contemporary accessories. Super7 Store (76) *(1628 Post St., 415-409-4700)* is packed with Japanese toys, vinyl figures, and T-shirts.

WHERE TO STAY

East meets West at Miyako Hotel (77) ($$–$$$) *(1625 Post St., 415-922-3200, www.miyakohotel.com)*. Rooms feature rice paper screens, bonsai, and Japanese tubs. Lavish furnishings at Victorian B&B Chateau Tivoli (78) ($$–$$$) *(1057 Steiner St., 415-776-5462, www.chateautivoli.com)* hail from great estates, including those of Charles de Gaulle, J. Paul Getty, and the Vanderbilts. Fluffy feather beds and noise-softening double-paned windows ensure a good night's rest at B&B Grove Inn (79) ($) *(890 Grove St., 415-929-0780, www.grovinn.com),* set in an Italianate Victorian home. Queen Anne Hotel (80) ($$–$$$) *(1590 Sutter St., 415-441-2828, www.queenanne.com)* comes with heirloom antiques and Miss Mary Lake, a friendly ghost. Hotel Majestic (81) ($$) *(1500 Sutter St., 415-441-1100, www.thehotelmajestic.com)* is also known for its resident ghost, the daughter of the building's first owner, along with its collection of African butterflies and Old World ambience.

chapter 5

PACIFIC HEIGHTS

COW HOLLOW/UNION STREET

THE MARINA

PACIFIC HEIGHTS
COW HOLLOW/UNION STREET
THE MARINA

Places to See:

1. Haas-Lilienthal House
2. Spreckels Mansion
3. Lyon Street Steps
4. Alta Plaza Park
5. Clay Theatre
26. Vedanta Temple
27. Octagon House
28. Golden Gate Valley Branch Library
29. Hourian Fine Art Galleries
30. Images of the North
56. Palace of Fine Arts
57. Wave Organ
58. Fort Mason Center

Places to Eat & Drink:

6. Quince
7. Elite Café
8. Vivande
9. Frankie's Bohemian Café
10. Ten-Ichi
11. Solstice Restaurant & Lounge
12. Harry's Bar
13. Lion Pub
14. G-Bar

31. Rose's Café
32. PlumpJack Café
33. Betelnut Pejiu Wu
34. Ottimista Enoteca-Café
35. Brazen Head
36. MatrixFillmore
37. Mauna Loa Club
38. Black Horse London Pub
59. Greens
60. Circa
61. Hime
62. A16
63. Isa
64. Nectar Wine Lounge
65. Zushi-Puzzle
66. Bistro Aix
67. Alegrias
68. Boboquivari's
69. HiFi
70. Kelley's Tavern
71. Monaghan's
72. Horseshoe Tavern
73. Final Final

Where to Shop:

15. Blu
16. HeidiSays

Where to Stay:

"You know what it is?
San Francisco is a golden handcuff
with the key thrown away."

—*John Steinbeck*

PACIFIC HEIGHTS

B: 1, 12, 22, 24, 27, 47, 49

• SNAPSHOT •

Soaring views and ever-soaring real estate prices mark the exclusive area known as Pacific Heights. Foreign consulates, finishing schools, Hollywood stars, socialites, and many of San Francisco's first families reside here. Stately mansions grace its hilltop setting, with sight lines reaching across the San Francisco Bay. The stretch along Broadway from Divisadero to Lyon streets, the "Gold Coast," offers particularly sweeping vistas. But not much existed on this sandy spot prior to the 1870s. The introduction of cable car lines on California, Clay, and later Washington streets eased access and sparked construction of Victorian houses. By the turn of the century, many were torn down in favor of period-style homes. Today tourists admire the mix: Victorian, Mission Revival, Edwardian, and *château* style. Many buildings fronting Lafayette and Alta Plaza parks are particularly ornate. An Upper Fillmore commercial corridor attracts serious shoppers to "Pac Heights" with boutiques, home design shops, and cafés.

PLACES TO SEE
Landmarks:

The **Haas-Lilienthal House (1)** *(2007 Franklin St., 415-441-3004)* is one of the area's architectural highlights. The rhapsodic 1886 Queen Anne with intricately-detailed gables is a museum and home of **San Francisco Architectural Heritage** *(www.sfheritage.org)*. Tours are available Sundays, Wednesdays, and Saturdays. **Spreckels Mansion (2)** *(2080 Washington St.)* was built for sugar fortune heir Adolph Spreckels and his wife Alma, the model for the Victory Monument in Union Square *(see page 62)*. The 55-room, white limestone mansion evokes a French Baroque palace. Novelist Danielle Steele and family reside here today. Get your heart racing in more ways than one by ascending the **Lyon Street Steps (3)** *(bet. Broadway and Green)*. Flanked by lush gardens and luxury homes, they lead to awesome views. You'll also enjoy the views from atop **Alta Plaza Park (4)** *(bordered by Scott, Jackson, Steiner, and Clay Sts.)*, designed by John McLaren, who landscaped Golden Gate Park. Pug dogs and their people gather here the first Sunday of every month for "Pug Sunday."

Arts & Entertainment:

The 1910 **Clay Theatre (5)** *(2261 Fillmore St., 415-267-4893, www.landmarktheatres.com)*, one of the city's oldest movie houses, screens independent films and foreign releases. It's also "Best Movie Theatre for Making Out," according to *San Francisco* magazine.

PLACES TO EAT & DRINK
Where to Eat:

Quince (6) ($$$) *(1701 Octavia St., 415-775-8500, www.quincerestaurant.com)* is one of the hottest tables in the city. Chef Michael Tusk melds Italian and French, creating sensations like Monterey Bay squid stuffed with artichoke, potato, and olives. Kick back with a Sazerac at **Elite Café (7) ($)** *(2049 Fillmore St., 415-673-5483, www.theelitecafe.com)*, where Louisiana bayou meets California fresh. The hearty menu includes meeting-house biscuits, jambalaya, and pulled pork with cheese grits and zucchini. Acclaimed **Vivande (8) ($$)** *(2125 Fillmore St., 415-346-4430, www.vivande.com)* brings authentic, artisanal Italian to the Heights. Its **Piccolo Wine Bar** offers small production, limited vintages. **Frankie's Bohemian Café (9) ($)** *(1862 Divisadero St., 415-921-4725)* tempts with tastes of the Czech Republic, like *brambory*, a potato/zucchini pancake with varied toppings. Fish is fresh at **Ten-Ichi (10) ($–$$)** *(2235 Fillmore St., 415-346-3477, tenichisf.com)*, a Fillmore mainstay. Vegetarians fare well here with tofu/vegetable stir-fry dishes and sukiyaki.

Bars & Nightlife:

Singles sip raspberry mojitos on purple ottomans while grooves spin at **Solstice Restaurant & Lounge (11)** *(2801 California St., 415-359-1222, www.solsticelounge.com)*. DJs kick it out Thursdays through Saturdays. **Harry's Bar (12)** *(2020 Fillmore St., 415-921-1000, www.harrys barsf.com)* brings in after-five business folk with a chill atmosphere and mixed drinks, including fruity mango mojitos. The bar serves a burger-and-fries style menu. **Lion Pub (13)** *(2062 Divisadero St., 415-567-6565)* steeps even more fruit in its famed strawberry/mango mojitos. A famous gay bar for decades, it now draws 20-something trendies. Seductive **G-Bar (14)** *(488 Presidio Ave., 415-409-4227; www.gbarsf.com)* recalls 1950s San Francisco. Sip a Gummi bear–garnished martini on a fireplace couch. Or go for the secluded Red Room, offering an Xbox, HDTV, and bottle service.

WHERE TO SHOP

Blu (15) *(2259 Fillmore St., 415-776-0643)* features European and name designers such as Martin Margiela. Other attractions: Barbara Bui shoes and voguish jewelry. A touch more affordable than some of its neighbors, **HeidiSays (16)** *(2426 Fillmore St., 415-749-0655, www.heidisays.com)* packs its racks with *au courant* feminine designers, like Trina Turk and Twelfth Street by Cynthia Vincent. Don't forget to stop by **HeidiSays Shoes** *(2105 Fillmore St., 415-409-6850)*. Western Addition meets Pacific Heights at **Boru Shop (17)**

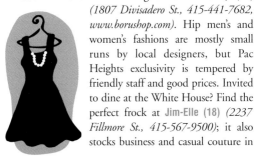

(1807 Divisadero St., 415-441-7682, www.borushop.com). Hip men's and women's fashions are mostly small runs by local designers, but Pac Heights exclusivity is tempered by friendly staff and good prices. Invited to dine at the White House? Find the perfect frock at **Jim-Elle (18)** *(2237 Fillmore St., 415-567-9500)*; it also stocks business and casual couture in

conservative styles. **Mrs. Dewson's Hats (19)** *(2050 Fillmore St., 415-346-1600, www.mrsdewsonhats.com)* have been worn by Hollywood stars and local politicians alike. Don't be shy about asking owner Ruth Garland Dewson to help select your new *chapeau*. **Browser Books (20)** *(2195 Fillmore St., 415-567-8027)* brings cerebral dimension to

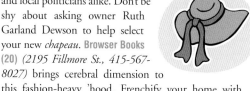

this fashion-heavy 'hood. Frenchify your home with Gallic accents from **Nest (21)** *(2300 Fillmore St., 415-292-6199)*, including quilts, antique beds, and chandeliers. It's hard to resist their gifts, jewelry, and purses. **Kiehl's (22)** *(2360 Fillmore St., 415-359-9260, www.kiehls.com)* uses animal-friendly, all-natural ingredients in its skin and hair care products. **Yountville (23)** *(2416 Fillmore St., 415-922-5050)* dresses girls from infant–size 8 and boys from infant–size 5. Expect appealing styles, inviting prices, and unique items, such as hand-embroidered booties.

WHERE TO STAY

At 1900 brownstone **Jackson Court (24) ($$)** *(2198 Jackson St., 415-929-7670, www.jacksoncourt.com)*, you'll find several rooms with fireplaces and a mix of antique and contemporary furnishings. Historic **Hotel Drisco (25) ($$)** *(2901 Pacific Ave., 415-346-2880, www.hoteldrisco.com)* offers accommodations in all flavors, including city-view and two-bedroom suites.

COW HOLLOW/UNION STREET

B: 22, 45

• SNAPSHOT •

Where dairy cows once grazed, shoppers now browse *chichi* boutiques and design stores. Cow Hollow, once known as Spring Valley and later Golden Gate Valley, is sandwiched between the Marina and Pacific Heights. This was dairy farmland and a fishermen's settlement before its coastline was filled in to build the Marina. Locals often include Cow Hollow when referring to the Marina. Today, neighborhood activity revolves around Union Street, where you'll find upscale retail spots, boisterous saloons, and picturesque Victorians.

PLACES TO SEE
Landmarks:

Though Northern California's Vedanta Society operates from a temple on Fillmore and Vallejo, it also owns Cow Hollow's **Vedanta Temple (26)** *(2963 Webster St., 415-922-2323, open Friday nights),* the West's first Hindu temple. Vedanta philosophy holds that all paths lead to the same god; the opulent 1905 structure reflects this inclusiveness with Moorish columns, Victorian details, and six unique domes, including a Russian-style onion-shaped dome. The **Octagon House (27)** *(2645 Gough St., 415-441-7512)* is one of only two left in the city. The eight-sided structures were thought to be more healthful for residents as they let in more light. The 1861 house originally stood across the street. It's now a museum of Colonial and Federal decorative arts. The San Francisco Public Library's **Golden Gate Valley Branch (28)** *(1801 Green St., 415-355-5666, sfpl.lib.ca.us)* was designed after a Roman basilica. The Beaux Arts structure was built in 1918 on land purchased by the city for $7,500 (about the same as one might easily spend now in a day of shopping on nearby Union Street).

Arts & Entertainment:

Hourian Fine Art Galleries (29) *(1843 Union St., 415-346-6400, www.hourianart.com)* features paintings and prints from European, Iranian, and U.S. artists, including works by owner Mohammad Hourian himself. **Images of the North (30)** *(2036 Union St., 415-673-1273, www.imagesnorth.com)* showcases compelling art by contemporary Inuit artists.

PLACES TO EAT & DRINK
Where to Eat:

Locals queue for Sunday brunch at **Rose's Café (31) ($$)** *(2298 Union St., 415-775-2200, www.rosescafesf.com)*, featuring breakfast pizzas with toppings like smoked salmon with *crème fraîche* and scrambled eggs. Sit out under the yellow awning, sip a mimosa, and watch the shoppers parade by. Sister spot **Terzo ($$)** *(3011 Steiner St., 415-441-3200, www.terzosf.com)* serves Pan-Med small plates. **PlumpJack Café (32) ($$)** *(3127 Fillmore St., 415-563-4755, www.plumpjackcafe.com)*, founded by city mayor Gavin Newsom, is a local favorite for its California cuisine and wine list. Boisterous **Betelnut Pejiu Wu (33) ($$)** *(2030 Union St., 415-929-8855, www.betelnutrestaurant.com)* serves Cal-Asian fusion cuisine, like chili-crusted calamari, five-spiced firecracker shrimp, and other Pan-Asian fare. Enjoy a "Mao-jiti" in its Dragonfly Lounge. The focus at **Ottimista Enoteca-Café (34) ($)** *(1838 Union St., 415-674-8400, www.ottimistasf.com)* is on little-known wine producers in Northern Italy and California. Vintages are paired with olives baked in pastry crust and other small bites. Old World décor and a heated patio boost the ambience. Burgers and French onion soup score points at **Brazen Head (35) ($$)** *(3166 Buchanan St., 415-921-7600, www.brazenheadsf.com)*, a pub-style spot that serves later than most.

Bars & Nightlife:

Historic **MatrixFillmore (36)** *(3138 Fillmore St., 415-563-4180, www.matrixfillmore.com)* is a top Cow Hollow spot. Janis Joplin, the Doors, and others performed at the original **Matrix Club**, opened by

Jefferson Airplane's Marty Balin. The current club is a classic pick-up scene with little room to breathe on weekends. Try midweek. **Mauna Loa Club (37)** *(3009 Fillmore St., 415-563-5137)* is a favorite watering hole; patrons enjoy foosball, pool, and Pop-a-Shot. Or skip the Marina scene and head to quirky **Black Horse London Pub (38)** *(1514 Union St., 415-928-2414, www.sfblack horsepub.com)*, the city's smallest, for a pint and a cheese plate. This relaxed spot swells to maximum capacity (22) on weekends.

WHERE TO SHOP

Even natives brave the crowds to shop at **Mingle (39)** *(1815 Union St., 415-674-8811, www.mingleshop.com)*, representing hot up-and-coming designers. Men will find some options here. **My Roommate's Closet (40)** *(3044 Fillmore St., 415-447-7703, www.myroom matescloset.com)*, a real find, sells names like Theory, Sass & Bide, and Vera Wang at discount prices. It's not a secondhand store, but an outlet for several exclusive boutiques. **Bryan Lee (41)** *(1840 Union St., 415-923-9923)* is all about helping patrons find the perfect denim fit. It also carries other fashions for men and women. Shoe fiends will swoon at **Shaw (42)** *(2001 Union St., 415-922-5676, www.shawshoes.net)*, where Italian designs might include Roberto Cavalli sandals with seashell-adorned straps. At **Workshop (43)** *(2254 Union St., 415-561-9551)* cashmeres and silks are works of art in themselves. Swimwear and lingerie are in a cottage out back. More like a museum than jewelry shop, sparkling Stuart Moore (44) *(1898 Union St., 415-292-1430, www.stuartmoore.com)* exhibits modern designs from 30 mostly European designers. Platinum and diamonds never looked so good. Sean (45) *(1749 Union St., 415-474-7363, www.seanstore.com)* carries Emile Lafaurie's impeccable French suits and signature poplin shirts. Looking for that dramatic, Philippe Starck–designed colander or stainless steel Swedish fireplace grate? ATYS (46) *(2149-B Union St., 415-441-9220, www.atysdesign.com)* home design store is the place. One of the city's top vintage showrooms, Past Perfect (47) *(2230 Union St., 415-929-7651)* has over 30 dealers; finds might include leather club chairs, a helium clown, clothing, and more. Gity Joon's (48) *(1828 Union St., 415-292-7388, www.gityjoon.com)* is worth a peek, even if you're not in the market for a Tibetan rug, Shiva statue, or Qing Dynasty double moon portal.

Kids:

Cool kids' boutique Wee Scotty (49) *(2266 Union St., 415-345-9200, www.weescotty.com)*, founded by rock designer Lynne Gallagher, offers children's sewing classes. Celeb clients include Madonna. Dress the progeny in

high-end duds at Mudpie (50) *(1694 Union St., 415-771-9262)*. Here, one-offs and French imports are the norm, as are big-time price tags. Downstairs, everything is half price. Moms, kids, and moms-to-be get the designer treatment at Minis (51) *(2278 Union St., 415-567-9537, www.minis-sf.com)*. Most of the Euro-style clothes are made exclusively for the store. Thursday's Child (52) *(1980 Union St., 415-346-1666)* is packed with *très chic* baby and pre-teen fashions and toys.

WHERE TO STAY

The recently redone Hotel Del Sol (53) ($$) *(3100 Webster St., 415-921-5520, www.thehoteldelsol.com)* has a splashy beach house feel. Each of the six rooms at B&B-style Union Street Inn (54) ($$–$$$) *(2229 Union St., 415-346-0424, www.unionstreetinn.com)* has its own theme. The most romantic: its Carriage House, with Jacuzzi for two, canopy bed, and private garden area. Edward II Bed & Breakfast (55) ($–$$) *(3155 Scott St., 415-922-3000, www.edwardii.com)* combines English décor with modern amenities. Rooms range from *pension* style with shared bath and gourmet breakfast to suites with Jacuzzi, sun porch, and garden.

THE MARINA

B: 22, 28, 30, 43

● SNAPSHOT ●

Something changes when you hit the Marina—the terrain becomes flat, and many residents resemble young Midwestern transplants. It wasn't always this way. Before 1989, an older population strolled Marina Green and patronized mom-and-pop shops. The Marina's backstory, shaped by the city's two biggest 20th-century earthquakes, has everything to do with the change. Originally, the area consisted of marshes and sand dunes. In 1906, the city began filling it in with earthquake rubble and made it the setting for the 1915 Panama-Pacific International Exposition world's fair. Less than a year later, the exposition buildings were torn down, save for the Palace of Fine Arts, which survives today. The area became prime real estate; a neighborhood was born. Turn the clock ahead to 1989 and the Loma Prieta Earthquake. The ground liquefied and structures crumbled; the old landfill foundation had

resulted in the Marina's sustaining more damage than any other neighborhood. Older residents got out. As the city rebuilt with new standards in earthquake construction, fresh-faced professionals streamed in, attracted by model homes, waterfront views, Marina Green, high-end shops, and trendy nightspots.

PLACES TO SEE
Landmarks:

The **Palace of Fine Arts (56)** *(3301 Lyon St., 415-567-6642, www.palaceoffinearts.org)*, a Neoclassical domed rotunda surrounded by a lagoon, is one of the city's architectural highlights. First constructed for the 1915 Panama-Pacific International Exposition, then used by the Army during WWII, the building fell into disrepair until restoration in the late 1960s. It now houses the **Exploratorium** *(see next page)* and **Palace of Fine Arts Theatre**, which hosts arts and cultural events.

Arts & Entertainment:

The otherwordly **Wave Organ (57)** *(end of Yacht Rd.)* combines unique public space with a sea-activated acoustic sculpture. Come at high tide and use the listening stations to catch its subtle sounds. **Fort Mason Center (58)** *(Marina Blvd., 415-441-3400, www.fortmason.org)*, located in Fort Mason itself, is the Marina's arts zone. Until 1962, the fort served as a military transport hub for armed forces during WWII and the Korean conflict. Now it's part of the Golden Gate National Recreation Area. Fort Mason Center comprises theaters, museums, a maritime library, and a radio station, and hosts exhibits, festivals, and performances. Its **Museo ItaloAmericano** *(Ft. Mason Ctr., Bldg. C, 415-673-2200, www.museoitaloamericano.org)* is devoted to Italian and Italian-American arts and culture. **San Francisco Museum of Modern Art Artists' Gallery** *(Ft. Mason Ctr., Bldg. A, 415-441-4777, www.sfmoma.org/museumstore/artists_overview.html)* represents more than 1,300 regional artists.

Kids:

The **Palace of Fine Arts (56)** **Exploratorium** *(3601 Lyon St., 415-EXP-LORE, 415-561-0360, www.exploratorium.edu)*, one of the world's first hands-on museums, offers hundreds of interactive exhibits. Reserve in advance for the popular Tactile Dome, where you're plunged into pitch darkness and must identify objects by touch.

PLACES TO EAT & DRINK
Where to Eat:
Greens (59) ($$) *(Ft. Mason Ctr., Bldg. A, 415-771-6222,*

www.greensrestaurant.com) was one of the first dining spots to bridge vegetarian and fine dining. Its organic produce comes from Marin County Zen Center's Green Gulch Farm. Elegant décor and Bay views are perfect complements. Be prepared for a wait at swank, small-plates **Circa (60) ($$)** *(2001 Chestnut St., 415-351-0175, www.circasf.com)*, offering new interpretations of classic dishes, such as

Tater Tots with Dungeness crab filling and lobster-truffle mac'n'cheese. Sushi sanctuary **Hime (61) ($$)** *(2353 Lombard St., 415-931-7900, www.himerestaurant.com)*, Japanese for "princess," treats patrons like royalty with its *izakaya*-style menu. The Marina crowd crams **A16 (62) ($$)** *(2355 Chestnut St. 415-771-2216, www.a16sf.com)* for Campania specialties like *maccaronara* with tomato ragu and ricotta. Some swear by the pizza. For one of the area's best culinary experiences, head to **Isa (63) ($–$$)** *(3324 Steiner St., 415-567-9588, www.isa restaurant.com)*, where chef Luke Sung brings French style to his small plates, succeeding with menu items such as truffled risotto and potato-wrapped sea bass. Sophisticated surrounds at **Nectar Wine Lounge (64) ($$)** *(3330 Steiner St., 415-345-1377, www.nectarwine lounge.com)* are conducive to conversing, while sipping one of its 50 varieties by the glass (800 by the bottle). Mouthwatering small plates enhance the experience. Refreshingly untrendy **Zushi-Puzzle (65) ($$)** *(1910 Lombard St., 415-931-9319, www.zushipuzzle.com)* delivers fresh sushi "fused with art." **Bistro Aix (66) ($$)** *(3340 Steiner St., 415-202-0100, www.bistroaix.com)* crosses several culinary styles in dishes from duck confit to tempura-fried calamari. Sit and sample wines on the patio. Want tapas without the over-the-top crowd? **Alegrias (67) ($-$$)** *(2018 Lombard St., 415-929-8888)* is the spot; it also dishes up delightful *flan*. **Boboquivari's (68) ($$$)** *(1450 Lombard St., 415-441-8880, www.boboquivari.com)* serves generous portions of dry-aged beef and whole crabs.

Bars & Nightlife:

Decked out in a retro lounge look, **HiFi (69)** *(2125 Lombard St., 415-345-8663, www.maximum productions.com)* buzzes with a rotating mix of DJs spinning rap, hip-hop, and '80s, '90s, and current grooves. **Kelley's Tavern (70)** *(3231 Fillmore St., 415-567-7181, www.kelleystavern.com)* is a singles magnet. Four screens here feature sports; one over the fireplace lets you watch from leather sofas. **Monaghan's (71)** *(3259 Pierce St., 415-567-4466)* gets its share of striped shirts and Financial District denizens, but it's a more relaxed setting to hang out, especially Mondays through Fridays. Touting itself as a "non-Marina" Marina bar, **Horseshoe Tavern (72)** *(2024 Chestnut St., 415-346-1430, www.horseshoetavernsf.com)* is down-to-earth friendly. "The Shoe" serves 15 beers on tap and gets busy during big games, when fans converge to watch TV. Play pool and darts and wash down free popcorn with beer at **Final Final (73)** *(2990 Baker St., 415-931-7800)*, local night owls' last stop before returning to multimillion-dollar homes in Marin County.

WHERE TO SHOP

Red Dot Chestnut (74) *(2176 Chestnut St., 415-346-0606, www.reddotshops.com)* sells cute clothes, shoes, and jewelry by names like Free People and Tulle. **Jack's (75)** *(2260 Chestnut St., 415-567-3673)* gives men a shot at haute couture with merchandise by Ted Baker, James Perse, and more, plus a Jack's Denim section. White walls at **Smash Shoes (76)** *(2030 Chestnut St., 415-673-4736)* accent high-fashion footwear from around the globe. Look for styles from Goffredo Fantini and Giuseppe Zanotti, among others.

WHERE TO STAY

America's Best Inn San Francisco (77) ($) *(2707 Lombard St., 415-567-2425, www.sanfranciscobi.com)* offers budget accommodations in a picturesque spot near the Presidio. Though set on busy Octavia Street, **Marina Inn (78) ($)** *(3110 Octavia St., 415-928-1000, www.marinainn.com)* has relatively quiet rooms recently updated in English country style. **Hostelling International San Francisco Fisherman's Wharf (79) ($)** *(Ft. Mason Ctr., Bldg. 240, 415-771-7277, www.sfhostels.com)* is an attractive hostel at Fort Mason; private rooms are available here for under $100.

chapter 6

★ *Top Picks*

"The Golden Gate Bridge's daily
striptease from enveloping stoles
of mist to full frontal glory is still the
most provocative show in town."

—*Mary Moore Mason*

THE PRESIDIO

B: 28, 29, 43, 76

• SNAPSHOT •

Sandwiched between the Marina and the exclusive Sea Cliff residential area, the Presidio ("fortress" in Spanish) is a former military outpost turned national park. Part of the Golden Gate National Recreation Area, the Presidio spans 1,400 acres and offers trails, two beach areas, and striking views of the Bay. It's also the gateway to the Golden Gate Bridge. On  the northern edge, a revamped Crissy Field runs along the waterfront. Here, San Franciscans flock on weekends for picnics, bike rides, jogging, and surfing.

PLACES TO SEE
Landmarks:

Clearly no visit to San Francisco is complete without a gander at or (better yet) a walk or bike ride across the ★GOLDEN GATE BRIDGE (1) *(U.S. Hwy. 101, 415-921-5858, www.goldengatebridge.org)*, the city's icon. Designed by Chicago engineer Joseph Strauss, the bridge debuted in May 1937 and was named one of the "Seven Wonders of the Modern World" by the American Society of Civil

TOP PICK!

Engineers in 1994. Painted in "International Orange" to match its natural setting and make it more visible in fog, the 1.7-mile bridge connects San Francisco with Marin County to the north. It's named after the Golden Gate Strait it towers over (which in turn was named after Istanbul's Golden Horn, the channel joining the Mediterranean with the Black Sea). During the bridge's construction, 11 men died when they fell, while 19 were saved by a safety net; the survivors formed an informal "Halfway to Hell Club." Today, a venerated crew of 55 stalwart painters and ironworkers maintain the bridge. Pedestrians are allowed on the east side. Bicyclists are allowed on both sides, but times vary *(check www.goldengatebridge.org/bikesbridge/bikes.php)*. It can be quite cold; dress in layers. Stop on the north side for city views and the **Lone Sailor Memorial** *(Vista Pt. exit,*

www.lonesailor.org/sf), commemorating members of the Navy, Marines, Coast Guard, and Merchant Marine who sailed out of the Golden Gate. The seven-foot statue of a sailor is a replica of artist Stanley Bleifeld's memorial in Washington, DC. The **Strauss Statue** in front of the Golden Gate Bridge Gift Center (15) *(see page 135)* on the southeast side depicts the bridge's chief engineer. **Fort Point (2)** *(end of Marine Dr., 415-561-4395, www.nps.gov/fopo)*, underneath the bridge, was constructed to guard the city from attack during the Civil War. Today, it offers exhibits, programs, and great views.

Boasting miles of beaches, bike routes, and hiking trails, the **Presidio** (*San Francisco Peninsula, 415-561-5300, www.presidio.gov*) was a military outpost controlled by Spain and then Mexico until 1848, when the U.S. claimed California. The Army managed the 1,491-acre area until the National Park Service took over in 1994. The park now mixes residential and commercial properties; plans call for it to be self-sustaining by 2013. Part of its funding comes from George Lucas's **Letterman Digital Arts Center** (*near Chestnut and Lyon*), the headquarters for Lucasfilm Ltd. **Inspiration Point (3)** (*inside the Arguello Blvd. gate*) offers amazing panoramas of the Presidio forest, the Bay, and Alcatraz. **Main Post** buildings mark the site of the original Spanish garrison and include the **Visitor Center (4)** (*50 Moraga Ave., 415-561-4323, www.presidio.gov/experiences/visitor.htm*) in the Mission-style **Officer's Club**. The **Presidio Golf Course (5)** (*300 Finley Rd., 415-561-4661, www.presidiogolf.com*), the second oldest west of the Mississippi, is known for its unique setting dotted with Monterey pines and eucalyptus trees. Rent a bike to make the most of a day in the park. The best views are along Lincoln Boulevard near the bridge toll plaza and "Pilot's Row," restored homes of 1920s Crissy Air Field pilots. **San Francisco National Cemetery (6)** (*150 Fisher Loop*), founded in 1884, is the resting place for 30,000 veterans, including 450 African American Buffalo Soldiers. **Crissy Field (7)** (*Presidio shoreline N. of Mason St., 415-561-7690, www.crissyfield.org*), site of the 1915 Panama-Pacific International Exposition, was revitalized in the late

1990s. More than 100,000 native plants were put in by community groups, and a promenade was constructed. The field is used by bikers and joggers; water rats enjoy sail- and kite-boarding. The first Burning Man festival was held at **Baker Beach (8)** *(western Presidio shoreline)*. It is unsafe for swimming, but offers views of the **Golden Gate Bridge (1)** *(see page 131)* and a protected picnic area. A popular nudist beach is located at its northern end. During the Gold Rush, **Mountain Lake (9)** *(12th Ave. and Lake St.)* provided fresh water for the city. Now it's part of a restful park that attracts ducks and local families.

Arts & Entertainment:

Arion Press (10) *(1802 Hays St., 415-668-2542, www.arionpress.com)* produces deluxe, hand-printed books that are among "the most beautiful" in the world, according to the *New York Times*. It has a gallery of limited edition books and prints, and offers Thursday tours. Call for reservations.

Kids:

Turn them loose at the **Julius Kahn Playground (11)** *(W. Pacific Ave. and Spruce St.)*, with swings and sandboxes.

PLACES TO EAT & DRINK
Where to Eat:

Go for soups, quesadillas, and pizza at **Acre Café (12) ($)** *(1013 Torney Ave., 415-561-2273)*, in the Thoreau Center for Sustainability. Sample international cuisine in bites or small plates at **Pres a Vi (13) ($$)** *(1 Letterman Dr., 415-409-3000, www.presavi.com)*. Wine and dessert connoisseurs can try new pairings, and a 22-seat chef's table lets you watch the action. **Presidio Social Club (14) ($-$$)** *(563 Ruger St., 415-885-1888, www.presidiosocialclub.com)* features American classics such as steak, oysters, and crab cakes.

WHERE TO SHOP

Golden Gate Bridge Gift Center (15) *(last San Francisco northbound exit off Hwy. 101; southbound, far right toll lane exit off 101, 415-923-2342, http://goldengate bridge.org/gift/)* offers souvenirs, books, and gifts. The 1938 roundhouse was originally a restaurant for motorists. Warming Hut (16) *(west end of Crissy Field, 415-561-3040)* sells sustainable light café fare, books, and gifts ranging from soy-wax candles to shade-grown coffee.

PRESIDIO HEIGHTS/ SACRAMENTO STREET

B: 1, 2, 3, 4, 33, 43

• SNAPSHOT •

More sophisticated than the Marina yet more casual than Pacific Heights, Presidio Heights and neighboring Laurel Heights exude money minus the flash. Well-tended Victorian homes and gardens border tree-lined streets. Moms maneuver strollers to upscale children's clothing stores or antique shops along Sacramento. Though nightlife is scarce, the low-key setting makes for an appealing atmosphere in which to wander and window-shop.

PLACES TO SEE
Landmarks:

Fires have played a major role in the city's history, with six great fires during the Gold Rush alone. The **San Francisco Fire Department Museum (17)** *(655 Presidio Ave., 415-563-4630, www.sffiremuseum.org)* tells the stories of the conflagrations and the heroes who fought them. The **Jewish Community Center of San Francisco (18)** *(3200 California St., 415-292-1200, www.jccsf. org)* has provided social and cultural programs since 1877. Landmark **Temple Emanu-El (19)** *(2 Lake St.,*

415-751-2535, www.emanuelsf.org), dedicated in 1926, is based on Istanbul's Hagia Sophia, and was named Northern California's finest work of architecture by the American Institute of Architects in 1927. Emanu-El has hosted Golda Meir, Martin Luther King, Jr., Elie Wiesel, Maya Angelou, and other notables.

Arts & Entertainment:

Tanzanian native Twiga of **Twiga Gallery (20)** *(3333 Sacramento St., 415-292-8020, www.twigagallery.com)* has amassed a museum-worthy collection of African antiques and tribal art pieces. She also sells her own handcrafted jewelry and home designs.

PLACES TO EAT & DRINK
Where to Eat:

Relax on the patio at romantic **Sociale (21) ($$)** *(3665 Sacramento St., 415-921-3200, www.caffe sociale.com)* and indulge in fontina-filled breaded olives or parsnip gnocchi with brown sage butter. The wine list includes rare Italian labels. **Garibaldis on Presidio (22) ($$-$$$)** *(347 Presidio Ave., 415-563-8841, www.garibaldisrestaurant.com)* mixes New York sophistication with West Coast warmth. Sip a pomegranate margarita and enjoy Cal-Med cuisine. Get in line for weekend brunch at **Ella's (23) ($)** *(500 Presidio Ave., 415-441-5669, www.ellassanfrancisco.com)*. The menu includes lemon ginger oatmeal pancakes and chicken hash. Baked goods made fresh daily.

WHERE TO SHOP

Grace & Co. Antiques (24) *(3440 Sacramento St., 415-567-5373, www.graceandcompanyantiques.com)* features 18th- and 19th-century American and English antiques, with some China Trade porcelain, clocks, paintings, and silver.

Feed your need for style at Grocery Store (25) *(3625 Sacramento St., 415-928-3615)*, catering to Miu Miu enthusiasts. You'll also find items by James Perse, Three Dots, and other labels. Button Down (26) *(3415 Sacramento St., 415-563-1311)* caters to men and women with Italian merchandise: Luciano Barbera blazers, silk scarves, cashmere slippers, and cufflinks. You'll find female fashion's most *chichi* names at Susan (27) *(3685 Sacramento St., 415-922-3685)*, including Galliano, Prada, and Marni. Many pieces are limited-run. Celebrated jeweler Margie Rogerson's by-appointment salon goldberry (28) *(3516 Sacramento St., 415-921-4389, www.goldberry.com)* custom-fits Burmese rubies, Colombian emeralds, Ceylon sapphires, and diamonds. For posh, pre-owned couture, try Designer Consigner (29) *(3525 Sacramento St., 415-440-8664)*; labels range from Ann Taylor to Versace and Chanel.

Kids:

Stroller-friendly Pumpkin (30) *(3366 Sacramento St., 415-567-6780, www.pumpkinbabes.com)* keeps kids in style with names like Diesel, Splendid, and Queen Bee. Dottie Doolittle (31) *(3680 Sacramento St, 415-563-3244, www.dottiedoolittle.com*) carries European and American labels for infants, girls to size 16, and boys to size 12, plus special-occasion attire. Young gents' haberdashery Martin Christopher (32) *(3490 Sacramento St., 415-673-3110, www.martinchristopher.com)*, stocks apparel by Hickey Freeman, Lochcarron, and Bobby Jones.

WHERE TO STAY

The Laurel Inn (33) ($$) *(444 Presidio Ave., 415-567-8467, www.thelaurelinn.com)* will make you feel at home with hip, studio-style rooms, some with views and kitchenettes.

"When you get tired of walking around San Francisco, you can always lean against it."

—*Author unknown*

INNER RICHMOND

B: 1, 2, 4, 21, 31, 33, 38, 44

• SNAPSHOT •

The shift from sand dunes to Chinese groceries has taken generations, but the Inner Richmond, once called a "Great Sand Waste," has become a bustling culinary and nightlife center. Part of the Richmond District, the area was developed in the late 19th century. Irish, Russian, and Jewish émigrés purchased homes here after WWI; then from the end of WWII to the 1950s, the Inner Richmond saw an influx of Japanese. A wave of Chinese led to the nickname "New Chinatown"—an estimated 35 percent of San Francisco's Chinese Americans live here. Asian restaurants, sushi bars, and bargain stores fill Geary Boulevard and Clement Street, its two main arteries, and students from nearby University of San Francisco frequent its bars. Despite its handful of boutiques and bistros, the neighborhood retains its working class roots.

PLACES TO SEE
Landmarks:

The Richmond area's former cemetery **Columbarium (34)** *(1 Loraine Ct., 800-445-3551, www.neptune-society. com/columbarium.shtml)* dates from 1889. The cremated remains of many prominent city residents are inurned within thousands of niches inside this three-story Victorian rotunda.

Arts & Entertainment:

Independent **Bridge Theatre (35)** *(3010 Geary Blvd., 415-267-4893, www.landmarktheatres.com)*, built in 1939, is one of the few single-screen theaters left in San Francisco. It's named after the Golden Gate Bridge, completed two years earlier.

PLACES TO EAT & DRINK
Where to Eat:

Clémentine (36) ($$) *(126 Clement St., 415-387-0408, www.clementine sf.com)* is a neighborhood haven with cosmopolitan cachet. Signature dishes include *escargots* Bourgogne and honey-roasted quail with *porcini*  ravioli. **Chapeau! (37) ($$)** *(1408 Clement St., 415-750-9787)* brings Gallic *gastronomie* to the Inner Richmond with its Provençal-style dining room and French-inspired fare, from *cassoulet* to duck *à l'orange* to chestnut soup. Bustling **Burma Superstar (38) ($)** *(309 Clement St., 415-387-2147, www.burmasuper star.com)* offers a mélange of Asian flavors, from hand-wrapped *samusas* to lemongrass salmon. Sushi disciples seeking pure forms of *unagi*, *toro*, and more head to **Murasaki Sushi Bar (39) ($$)** *(211 Clement St., 415-668-7317, www.murasaki-sushi.com)* for their fish fix. Come to **Katia's (40) ($-$$)** *(600 5th Ave., 415-668-9292, www.katias.com)* for tea, lunch, brunch, or dinner. The accordionist covers rock hits, Russian beer flows, and Chef Katia Troosh dishes out *blini*, *pelmeni*,

and *borscht*. **Schubert's Bakery (41) ($)** *(521 Clement St., 415-752-1580, www. schuberts-bakery.com)*, one of the city's oldest, dazzles patrons with mango mousse cake and other confections.

Bars & Nightlife:

540 Club (42) *(540 Clement St., 415-752-7276, www.540-club.com)* is popular for its indie-style jukebox and DJs, as well as Monday Night Dollar Drinks. Rotating art exhibits include rock poster and tattoo designs. Soju is the drink of choice at **RoHan Lounge (43)** *(3809 Geary Blvd., 415-221-5095, www.rohanlounge.com)*, mostly in inventive, super-sweet cocktails. This hip-urban nightspot also features DJs and late-night Pan Asian tapas. **Plough & Stars (44)** *(116 Clement St., 415-751-1122, www.the ploughandstars.com)* is considered one of the city's most authentic Irish pubs. Sip Irish coffee, quaff a Guinness, and enjoy live music, from fiddlers to Celtic rock.

WHERE TO SHOP

Antique Traders (45) *(4300 California St., 415-668-4444, www.theantiquetraders.com)* sells Art Nouveau lamps, stained glass, and art glass pieces, including Tiffany and Galle. Leather artisan Beatrice Amblard uses **April in Paris (46)** *(55 Clement St., 415-750-9910, www.aprilinparis.us)* to showcase her works, from saddle-stitched handbags to belts. San Franciscans love **Green Apple Books & Music (47)** *(506 Clement St., 415-387-2272, www.greenapplebooks.com)*, packed with used books, bestsellers, bargain overstocks, and magazines. Its **Fiction & Music Annex** stocks CDs, DVDs, and audio books. Tiny **Vinh Khang Herb & Ginseng (48)** *(512 Clement St., 415-752-8336)* brims with beneficial herbs. Its claim to fame: Julia Roberts shopped here while filming *Dying Young*. **Period George (49)** *(7 Clement St., 415-752-1900)* carries 18th- and 19th-century antiques, mostly fine china and glassware, found on owner Donald Gibson's travels to Asia and Europe. Eclectic defines gift trove **Kumquat Art & Home (50)** *(9 Clement St., 415-752-2140, www.kumquatart.com)*, selling "happy, friendly art" and accessories; half its stock is by local artists. Japanophiles converge at **Heroes Club (51)** *(840 Clement St., 415-387-4552, www.artoftoy.com)* for full action figures and limited-edition collectibles.

OUTER RICHMOND/LAND'S END

B: 1, 2, 5, 18, 31, 38

• SNAPSHOT •

The Outer Richmond is located in the midst of the city's premier parks and real estate, with the Presidio, Sea Cliff, and Lincoln Park to its north and Golden Gate Park to the south. Called "The Avenues" by locals for its numbered avenues running north/south, the area, a 19th-century cemetery site, was used for emergency housing after the 1906 earthquake. Many victims chose to stay on, then Jewish and Irish immigrants soon filled the area. Chinese newcomers joined them in the 1950s, but the neighborhood is now home to a large Russian community as well, many having arrived in the 1990s after the fall of the Soviet Union. Today the Outer Richmond, though mostly residential, has international restaurants, a world-class museum, and a park that (when free of fog) lends superb ocean views. Fog is indeed a big factor here, especially in summer, when it gets downright blustery.

PLACES TO SEE

Landmarks:

Cliff House (52) *(1090 Pt. Lobos Ave., 415-386-3330, www.cliffhouse.com)*, known for its spectacular Pacific vistas, has had three incarna-

tions. The first, built in 1863, was frequented by presidents and the wealthy. Entrepreneur and one-time city mayor Adolph Sutro purchased it in 1881; 13 years later, it burned down on Christmas Day. Sutro erected a grander, French château-style version; it, too, was destroyed by fire. Sutro's daughter, Emma, rebuilt in 1909 with a Neoclassical design. This structure, now part of the Golden Gate National Recreation Area, houses two popular restaurants and a brunch/party room. To the north are the eerie ruins of the **Sutro Baths** *(www.nps.gov/goga/clho.htm)*. Built in 1896, they rivaled the ancient baths of Rome, with seven swimming pools under glass, six of which could fill within an hour at high tide, as well as over 500 dressing rooms, restaurants, galleries, and an amphitheater. The complex later became an ice rink; it was destroyed by fire in 1966. Stone lions stand watch at windswept **Sutro Heights Park (53)** *(Pt. Lobos Ave.)*, once the site of Adolph Sutro's mansion. Curious **Camera Obscura (54)** *(lower terrace behind Cliff House, 415-750-0415, www.giant camera.com)*, a giant camera based on a design by Leonardo da Vinci, was built in 1946. It's housed in a yellow structure shaped like a camera itself. Step inside for live panoramic views of **Seal Rocks (55)**. At one time these rocks were covered with boisterous sea lions; after the 1989 Loma Prieta Earthquake, many moved to Pier 39 *(see page 24)*. Some seals still call the rocks home, as do a variety of birds. **Lincoln Park (56)** *(entrance 34th Ave. and Clement St.)*, like much of the Richmond, was a

cemetery in the late 1800s. After the cemetery was relocated, the park's small golf course was expanded by golf architect Tom Bendelow. Today, **Lincoln Park Golf Course** *(300 34th Ave., 415-221-9911, www.playlincoln golf.com)* is famed for its 17th hole views of Golden Gate Bridge. The park is also the site of sculptor George Segal's **Holocaust Memorial**; the tableau depicts ten bodies and a standing figure with one hand raised at a barbed wire fence. Several scenic trails, including the revitalized **Coastal Trail**, mark **Land's End (57)**. Though the water is brisk, **China Beach (58)** *(25th Ave., left on Seacliff Ave.)* is safe for swimming.

Arts & Entertainment:

Commemorating California soldiers who died in WWI, and modeled after Paris's Palais de la Légion d'Honneur, the Beaux Arts **California Palace of the Legion of Honor (59)** *(34th Ave. in Lincoln Park, 415-863-3330, www.legionofhonor.org)* boasts a dramatic clifftop setting and outstanding collections of European and ancient art, works on paper, porcelain, and more.

PLACES TO EAT & DRINK
Where to Eat:

A meal at one of the **Cliff House (52)** *(1090 Point Lobos Ave., 415-386-3330, www.cliffhouse.com)* restaurants is always memorable. Try **Sutro's ($$-$$$)** for coastal cuisine featuring local organic ingredients. **Bistro ($$)** serves omelets, sandwiches, and *cioppino*, the city's famed fish stew. And the **Terrace Room Sunday Champagne Brunch ($$)** is always a sellout; reserve ahead *(415-386-3330)*. Leave your shoes at the door and enjoy relaxed cushion seating at **Khan Toke Thai House (60) ($-$$)** *(5937 Geary Blvd., 415-668-6654)*. Wood carvings, tapestries, a garden, and the Thai wait staff's traditional dress add to the ambience. When the fog sets in, go for piping hot bowls of *pho* and juicy plates of peppercorn crab at **PPQ Dungeness Island (61) ($)** *(2332 Clement St., 415-386-8266, www.ppqdungeness.com)*. Or warm up Peruvian style at **Karamanduka (62) ($$)** *(1801 Clement St., 415-422-0502), www.karamanduka.com)*. Try *ceviche de camaron a la plancha*: prawn ceviche in a clay pot with garlic, vodka-infused ginger sugarcane, fried yucca, and yams. **Al-Masri (63) ($$)** *(4031 Balboa St., 415-876-2300, www.almasrirestaurant.com)*, "The Egyptian," will whisk you to the land of the Nile with authentic belly dancing and exotic delicacies. **Aziza (64) ($$)** *(5800 Geary Blvd., 415-752-2222, www.aziza-sf.com)* awakens the senses with candles, cocktails, and Chef Mourad Lahlou's Moroccan cuisine. **Joe's Ice Cream**

(65) ($) *(5351 Geary Blvd., 415-751-1950, www.joesice cream.com)* has been scooping since 1959. Enjoy old-school flavors and fresh new ones, like green tea and adzuki bean.

Bars & Nightlife:

Tiki bar **Trad'r Sam (66)** *(6150 Geary Blvd., 415-221-0773)* combines lethal cocktails with divey ambience. Slip into a "Scorpion Bowl" (after designating your driver).

WHERE TO SHOP

Arguably one of the largest collections (over 5,000) of Limoges porcelain boxes is found at Gaslight & Shadows (67) *(2335 Clement St., 415-387-0633, www.boxeslimoges.com)*. Mini

Muzzy's Attic (68) *(3448 Balboa St., 415-831-4338, www.muzzysattic.com)* is packed with unique treasures, from antique armoires to cast-iron cookware. Kimberley's Consignment Couture (69) *(3020 Clement St., 415-752-2223, www.kimberleyssf.com)* offers new and nearly new fashions by Chanel, Jil Sander, Prada, and Hermès. Miranda's Mama (70) *(3785 Balboa St., 415-221-5862, www.mirandasmama.com)* stocks preowned infant and children's clothes, toys, and more, plus maternity items.

WHERE TO STAY

Seal Rock Motor Inn (71) ($) *(545 Pt. Lobos Ave., 415-752-8000, www.sealrockinn.com)* is one of the city's best bargains, especially for families (and gonzo journalists—Hunter S. Thompson stayed here). Large rooms provide Pacific views; many have fireplaces. The cookie jar is always full at **Ocean Beach Bed & Breakfast (72) ($-$$)** *(611 42nd Ave., 415-668-0193, www.bbhost.com/ocean beach)*, offering an Ocean View Suite for up to four and a Queen Room for singles or couples.

"I have always been better treated in San Francisco than I actually deserved."

—*Mark Twain*

chapter 7

GOLDEN GATE PARK

INNER SUNSET

OUTER SUNSET/PARKSIDE

GOLDEN GATE PARK
INNER SUNSET
OUTER SUNSET/PARKSIDE

Places to See:

1. McLaren Lodge
2. Conservatory of Flowers
3. San Francisco Botanical Garden
4. Garden of Shakespeare's Flowers
5. Japanese Tea Garden
6. Stow Lake
7. Spreckels Lake
8. Buffalo Paddock
9. Dutch Windmill
10. Murphy's Windmill
11. Kezar Stadium
12. Music Concourse
13. Portals of the Past
14. National AIDS Memorial Grove
15. de Young Museum
16. Golden Gate Park Golf Course
17. Koret Children's Quarter
19. Grand View Park
20. St. Anne of the Sunset Church
21. Canvas Gallery
35. Ocean Beach

36. Fort Funston
37. Lake Merced
38. Harding Park Golf Course
39. Doggie Diner Dachshund Head
40. Stern Grove and Pine Lake Park
41. San Francisco Zoo

Places to Eat & Drink:

18. Beach Chalet Brewery & Restaurant
22. Park Chow
23. PJ's Oyster Bed
24. Ebisu
25. New Eritrea
26. San Tung Chinese Restaurant #2
27. Dragonfly
28. Arizmendi Bakery
29. Art's Café
30. Little Shamrock
42. Ristorante Marcello
43. Pisces California Cuisine
44. Marnee Thai
45. Thanh Long
46. So

"What fetched me instantly…
was the subtle but unmistakable sense
of escape from the United States."

—H. L. Mencken

GOLDEN GATE PARK

B: 5, 7, 18, 21, 28, 29, 33, 44, 71
Muni N-Judah line to Stanyan or 9th Ave.

• SNAPSHOT •

New York has its Central Park, Paris its Tuileries. But nothing compares with the engineering feat that transformed 1,000 acres of desolate sand dunes into miles of meadows, lakes, forests, and gardens. The idea for an urban park in San Francisco took shape during the Gold Rush; its nouveau riche sought to enhance the community. Add a population boom, and the metropolis was ready for restorative green space. ★**GOLDEN GATE PARK** *(bordered by Great Highway, Fulton and Stanyan Sts., and Lincoln Wy., www.parks.sfgov.org)* exists on the former Great Sand Bank, a stretch of land even Frederick Law Olmsted (Central Park's famed designer) did not think could be converted. Engineer William Hammond Hall began construction on the park in 1870, but it was unconventional Scots-born superintendent John McLaren who would flesh out the plan; during his 1890–1943 tenure, the passionate gardener planted more than a

TOP PICK!

million trees! Today, the park is home to world-class museums, vibrant gardens, a fly-casting pool, a golf course, even a herd of buffalo. John F. Kennedy Drive, one of the park's main thorough-fares, is partially closed to vehicles on Sundays in favor of bikers, rollerbladers, and joggers. That said, it's difficult to see all the park has to offer without a car, though public transportation will get you close; once there, San Francisco Parks Trust offers free walking tours *(call 415-263-0991)*.

PLACES TO SEE
Landmarks:

Although the best way to absorb the spirit of **Golden Gate Park** is by ambling through it, there are key attractions you won't want to miss. A good first stop for visitor information is Park Headquarters, **McLaren Lodge (1)** *(JFK Dr., 415-831-2700)*, John McLaren's former home. Note: You'll find another visitor center on the Pacific end of the park in **Beach Chalet Brewery & Restaurant (18)** *(see page 157)*. Walk west until you reach the dazzling **Conservatory of Flowers (2)** *(JFK Dr., 415-666-7001, www.conservatoryofflowers.org)*, North America's oldest public conservatory. Set in a Victorian glass palace, it opened in 1879 and survived the 1906 earthquake. A devastating 1995 winter storm closed

the conservatory for eight years. It reopened with five galleries of rare and exotic plants and flowers, including a century-old imperial philodendron, giant water lilies, and hundreds of species of orchids. The 55-acre **San Francisco Botanical Garden (3)** *(9th Ave. at Lincoln Way, 415-661-1316, www.sfbotanicalgarden.org)* at **Strybing Arboretum** fea-

tures over 7,500 varieties of plants. Its collections include cloud forests, a redwood trail, primitive plant garden, and a Japanese moon-viewing garden. Other park gardens include a **Garden of Shakespeare's Flowers (4)** *(MLK Dr. and Middle Dr. E.)*, showcasing herbs, plants, and flowers mentioned in the Bard's works, and the popular **Japanese Tea Garden (5)** *(bet. JFK and MLK Drs., 415-752-4227)*, created for an 1894 world's fair; it includes a five-story pagoda, bonsai and cherry trees, waterfalls, bridges, and a large bronze Buddha cast in 1790. Its Tea House serves tea and cookies. For views of the park, climb 428-foot **Strawberry Hill**, surrounded by picturesque **Stow Lake (6)** *(Stow Lake Dr.)*. Rent paddle-boats through **Stow Lake Boat & Bike Rentals** *(50 Stow Lake Dr., 415-752-0347)*. **Spreckels Lake (7)** *(near 36th Ave., north side of park)* is the venue of choice for model yacht enthusiasts. The **Buffalo Paddock (8)** *(JFK Dr.)* houses a small herd of bison. At one time, the park was irrigated with water pumped by the **Dutch Windmill (9)** *(west end of the park)* next to the **Queen Wilhelmina Tulip Garden** and **Murphy's Windmill (10)** *(southwest corner)*. **Kezar Stadium (11)** *(755 Stanyan St., southeast corner)* is the birthplace of the San Francisco 49ers and Oakland Raiders football teams. Today, it hosts lacrosse, soccer, and other local sports. The landmark **Music Concourse (12)** *(Tea Garden Dr.)* dates from the 1894 International

Exposition. It includes a band shell for live performances and seating amid hundreds of trees planted in a grid pattern to provide shade. The last Nob Hill structure standing after the 1906 earthquake was the columned entryway of the A.N. Towne mansion; you'll find it today at **Portals of the Past (13)** *(Lloyd Lake, JFK Dr.)*. The fern-, pine-, and redwood-filled **National AIDS Memorial Grove (14)** *(Bowling Green Dr. and Middle Dr. E., 415-750-8340, www.aidsmemorial.org)* was designed in 1988 as a living memorial to San Franciscans and others who have succumbed to AIDS.

Arts & Entertainment:

The **de Young Museum (15)** *(50 Hagiwara Tea Garden Dr., 415-863-3330, www.deyoungmuseum.org)*, named after a former *San Francisco Chronicle* editor and museum founder, opened in 1895. Its current facility, an über-modern structure lined with copper plates, opened in 2005. Galleries include collections of American art from the 17th to 20th centuries, and Native American, African, and Pacific art. Golfers practice strokes at **Golden Gate Park Golf Course (16)** *(970 47th Ave., 415-751-8987)*, a nine-hole public venue amid stands of eucalyptus.

Kids:

The park's just-refurbished **Koret Children's Quarter (17)** *(MLK Dr. and Bowling Green Dr.)* playground aims to provide a "safe, imaginative, adventurous" place for kids. The playground is home to a 1912 Herschell-Spillman carousel.

PLACES TO EAT & DRINK
Where to Eat:

Beach Chalet Brewery & Restaurant (18) ($$) *(1000 Great Hwy., 415-386-8439, www.beachchalet.com)* is a favorite for its American cuisine, ales, and ocean views. The downstairs **Golden Gate Park Visitor's Center** features 1930s frescoes and woodcarvings and offers park information. Views at sister eatery **Park Chalet Garden Restaurant ($)** *(1000 Great Hwy., 415-386-8439, www. beachchalet.com)* showcase the park rather than the ocean. A fireplace and retractable glass doors and ceiling raise the hip factor here; casual dining emphasizes barbecue and pizza options. Both places have live music most nights.

INNER SUNSET

B: 6, 28, 44, 71
Muni N-Judah line to 9th Ave. and Irving or Judah

• SNAPSHOT •

One of the last chunks of the city to be developed, the Sunset District sprawls from Cole Valley's edge out to the Pacific, an area besieged by fog during summer. Some say its incongruous name was part of the sales strategy of a developer who built homes here in the late 1800s. Irish immigrants who cared more about affordable housing than dreary weather moved in, as did the University of California Medical Center. Asian immigrants opened restaurants, laundromats, five-and-dimes, and produce stands, creating an international enclave, mostly around 9th and Irving. Though it has no major attractions, the Inner Sunset's appeal is its sense of community. Residents know shop owners and attempt, albeit not always successfully, to keep big chains out. Despite rising real estate prices, mom-and-pops hang on, quirky gift stores thrive on foot traffic, and college kids liven up cafés and bars.

PLACES TO SEE
Landmarks:

Grand View Park (19) *(Moraga St., 15th and 14th Aves., and Noriega St.)* offers just that. Two sets of staircases take you to paths that lead to the peak of 820-foot "Turtle Hill." When the fog clears, Golden Gate Park, both city bridges, and the Pacific are in view. It's hard to miss the peach-pink, Mission-style twin towers of **St. Anne of the Sunset Church (20)** *(850 Judah St., 415-665-1600, www.stanne-sf.org)*. The 1931 church celebrates mass in Arabic and Cantonese.

Arts & Entertainment:

Progressive culture venue and café/lounge **Canvas Gallery (21)** *(1200 9th Ave., 415-504-0060, www.thecanvas gallery.com)* showcases new talent in music and enter-tainment and is considered one of the city's best places to buy art. Its monthly **Feria Urbana** ("urban fair") offers clothing, jewelry, and home accessories.

PLACES TO EAT & DRINK
Where to Eat:

Comfort foodies chow down at **Park Chow (22) ($)** *(1240 9th Ave., 415-665-9912)*. Sit on the patio, by the fire-place, or at the bar. Menu favorites: Cobb salad, Thai noodles, wood-fired pizza, pork chops, French toast, and ginger cake with pumpkin ice cream. A mainstay along busy Irving, **PJ's Oyster Bed (23) ($$)** *(737 Irving St., 415-566-7775, www.pjsoysterbed.com)* brings New

Orleans to the Sunset with Creole jambalaya, "Voodoo Shrimp," and desserts like "Devastating Swamp Pie." Its **Big Easy Lounge** features Fat Wednesday $2 oyster shooters. If you don't mind a wait, **Ebisu (24) ($$)** *(1283 9th Ave., 415-566-1770, www.ebisusushi.com)* delivers fresh fish and rolls that have earned multiple awards. Its sushi samplers are a good value. The Ethiopian-style *injera* bread and savory toppings at understated **New Eritrea**

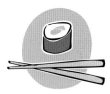

(25) ($) *(907 Irving St., 415-681-1288)* are some of the best in the city. At **San Tung Chinese Restaurant #2 (26) ($)** *(1031 Irving St., 415-242-0828)* the lights are too bright and the décor a bit dull, but patrons don't notice. They're too busy devouring noodle dishes, chicken wings, and dim sum specialties. Upscale **Dragonfly (27) ($-$$)** *(420 Judah St., 415-661-7755)* adds a touch of sleek and modern to Vietnamese dining. Early risers come to **Arizmendi Bakery (28) ($)** *(1331 9th Ave., 415-566-3117, www.arizmendibakery.org)* for scones, cheese rolls, and provolone-olive bread. Art of **Art's Café (29) ($)** *(747 Irving St., 415-665-7440)* and his wife have operated this sliver of a diner since the 1940s. Customers rave about the hash browns, *kim chee* omelets, and Korean barbecue.

Bars & Nightlife:

Little Shamrock (30) *(807 Lincoln Way, 415-661-0060)* is one of the city's oldest bars; the hands of its clock are stuck at the hour it stopped after the 1906 earthquake.

With free popcorn, beers on tap, Irish whiskey, board games, a crackling fire, and comfy couches, this is the place to spend a foggy night.

WHERE TO SHOP

Black Oak Books (31) *(630 Irving St., 415-564-0877, www.blackoakbooks.com)* is hands down the tidiest used bookshop around. A student haunt for its textbooks, the shop also has a selection of new titles. Designer Catherine Jane (32) *(1234 9th Ave., 415-664-1855, www.catherinejane.net)* accentuates the feminine with smart pencil skirts, floral dresses, and classic wrap tops. She also carries accessories and sexy footwear. Tutti Frutti (33) *(718 Irving St., 415-661-8504)* jams every corner of its space with quirky knickknacks and toys. Think boxing nuns, funky gift books, and bobbleheads. Wishbone (34) *(601 Irving St., 415-242-5540, www.wishbonesf. com)* offers more whimsy: Paul Frank paraphernalia, Gama-Go T-shirts, fun baby gear, greeting cards, and more.

OUTER SUNSET/PARKSIDE

B: 18, 29, 48, 71
Muni L-Taraval and N-Judah lines to Great Highway

• SNAPSHOT •

Traveling to the tranquil Sunset District may make you feel as if you're venturing into a world outside San Francisco with grids of family homes as far as the eye can see. The Outer Sunset, also called "The Avenues," was developed between the 1920s and 1950s. Though it stretches from 19th Avenue to Ocean Beach, most eateries run about ten blocks along the Irving Street corridor, starting at 19th. The Parkside subdivision, south of the Outer Sunset, is almost a neighborhood of its own. A commercial strip lined with restaurants and cafés runs along Taraval from 15th to about 30th avenues. Aside from the cultural mix, the main attractions here are natural ones: Ocean Beach to the west, Lake Merced to the south, and Stern Grove on the southeast edge.

PLACES TO SEE
Landmarks:

Spanning just over three miles, **Ocean Beach (35)** *(along Great Highway)* is the city's longest. Its frigid temperatures and rip currents befit seasoned surfers who congregate in insulated wetsuits near the north end. For much of the summer, fog envelops the beach, making for a desolate landscape. When it breaks during the warmer months of September and October, the beach fills with sunbathers; kite fliers and boarders come to take advantage of the winds. Windswept **Fort Funston (36)** *(Skyline Blvd., 415-556-8371, 415-561-4323)* park, a former military reservation, is a favorite of dogs, dog owners, hang gliders, and hikers. Enjoy a walk along its paved **Sunset Trail** loop. **Lake Merced (37)** *(off Skyline Blvd.)*, originally named "Lake of Our Lady of Mercy" by the Spanish in the 1700s, is ringed by a 4.5-mile road used by joggers and bikers. The area is also home to the newly renovated **Harding Park Golf Course (38)** *(99 Harding Rd., 415-664-4690, www.harding-park.com)*, designed by Willie Watson in 1925. The cypress-dotted lakeshore setting has made this one of the U.S.'s most popular municipal courses. The **Doggie Diner Dachshund Head (39)** *(Sloat Blvd. near Ocean Beach)* once promoted a "Doggie Diner" fast-food chain. The diners are long closed, but the restored 700-pound pup remains, thanks to dogged preservation efforts by the community.

Arts & Entertainment:

Stroll 64 ethereal acres of eucalyptus, redwoods, and firs at **Stern Grove** and **Pine Lake Park (40)** *(19th Ave. and Sloat Blvd.)*. The Stern Grove Festival *(see page 17)* concert series is a summer "must-do."

Kids:

San Francisco Zoo (41) *(1 Zoo Rd., 415-753-7080, www.sfzoo.org)*, formerly the Herbert Fleishhacker Zoo after its founder, began in 1889 with the capture of a grizzly bear named Monarch. Highlights: a new Lemur Forest, African Savanna, Penguin Island, and Children's Zoo. The zoo is also home to a 1921 Dentzel carousel and a Little Puffer historic miniature steam train.

PLACES TO EAT & DRINK
Where to Eat:

The fifties-style ambience at Parkside mainstay **Ristorante Marcello (42) ($$)** *(2100 Taraval St., 415-665-1430)* sets the stage for Tuscan-influenced meat entrées, seafood platters, homemade pasta, and a California and Italian wine list. **Pisces California Cuisine (43) ($)** *(3414 Judah St., 415-564-2233)* uses organic greens and local ingredients where possible and serves a mean bowl of *cioppino*. The homestyle Central Thai dishes at **Marnee Thai (44) ($)** *(2225 Irving St., 415-665-9500, www.marneethaisf.com)* have been winning raves for 20 years. Top off a day at the beach with a roasted crab and garlic noodles at popular **Thanh Long (45) ($$-$$$)** *(4101 Judah St., 415-665-1146, www.anfamily.com)*. The college-aged crowd comes to **So (46) ($)** *(2240 Irving St., 415-731-3143)*

for homemade pot stickers, heaping noodle dishes, and soju cocktails. **Old Mandarin Islamic Restaurant (47) ($)** *(3132 Vicente St., 415-564-3481)* gives northern Chinese cuisine a Muslim twist. The lamb soup hot pot is a favorite. At **Yum Yum Fish (48) ($)** *(2181 Irving St., 415-566-6433, www.yumyumfishsushi.com)*, the name pretty much says it all. Half fish market, half sushi joint, it serves daily catch and rolls at wholesale prices. Peak-time waits are inevitable for the few tables. Some of the city's finest gelato is scooped at **Marco Polo Italian Ice Cream (49) ($)** *(1447 Taraval St., 415-731-2833)*. The shop adds an Asian edge with flavors like lychee, red bean, mango, and controversial durian. **Feel Real Organic Vegan Café (50) ($)** *(4001 Judah St., 415-504-7325)* is one of the city's most laid-back dining experiences, complete with sliding-scale prices. Be prepared for a wait for the "Homegrown" (veggie burger), the passion salad, or a ginger coconut cookie. Reggae music rules; kitchen workers sing along. When the sun makes an appearance, surfers, locals, and tourists claim outdoor seats at **Java Beach Café (51) ($)** *(1396 La Playa St., 415-665-5282, www.javabeachcafe.com)*. After the fog returns, everyone heads inside for coffee, sandwiches, soup, or a pint.

Bars & Nightlife:

Riptide (52) *(3639 Taraval St., 415-681-8433, www.rip tidesf.com)*, with its knotty pine, moose head, and fire-

place, more resembles a mountain lodge than a city dive. DJs, live music, bargain beers, and an ocean-view patio are all part of its appeal. **Durty Nelly's (53)** *(2328 Irving St., 415-664-2555)* brings a bit of the Emerald Isle to Asia-centric Irving Street. Despite its name, the pub has the right elements: cozy fire, wooden booths, and menu items like shepherd's pie. Convivial Irish ex-pats fill the space.

WHERE TO SHOP

Outer Sunset surfers shop cool Mollusk Surf Shop (54) *(4500 Irving St., 415-564-6300, www.mollusksurf shop.com)* for boards, accessories, and art, or friendly Aqua Surf Shop (55) *(2830 Sloat Blvd., 415-242-9283, www.aquasurfshop.com)*, featuring ebullient shop dog, Merle. A Happy Planet (56) *(4501 Irving St., 415-753-8300, www.ahappyplanet.com)* sells organic pillows, sheets, comforters, and undergarments for the family.

WHERE TO STAY

Comfortable seaside accommodations come at value prices at family-friendly Great Highway Inn (57) ($-$$) *(1234 Great Hwy., 415-731-6644, www.greathwy.com)*. The third floor offers Pacific views. Some of the rooms at Oceanview Motel (58) ($) *(4340 Judah St., 415-661-2300, www.oceanviewmotel.citysearch.com)* also offer ocean views. This no-frills spot was recently upgraded. As one reviewer said, "Leave your heart but not your wallet" at Ocean Park Motel (59) ($) *(2690 46th Ave., 415-566-7020, www.oceanparkmotel.citysearch.com)*; the Art Deco delight opened the same year as the Golden Gate Bridge and claims to be San Francisco's first motel.

"San Francisco is forty-nine square miles surrounded by reality."

—Paul Kantner, Jefferson Airplane

chapter 8

```
┌─────────────────────────────────┐
│                                 │
│        THE HAIGHT               │
│       COLE VALLEY               │
│        THE CASTRO               │
│       NOE VALLEY                │
│                                 │
└─────────────────────────────────┘
```

Places to See:

1. Haight and Ashbury
2. Grateful Dead House
3. Buena Vista Park
4. Red Vic Movie House
36. Tank Hill
47. Harvey Milk Plaza
48. Pink Triangle Park
    and Memorial
49. Castro Theatre
50. Randall Museum
73. Twin Peaks
74. Golden Fire Hydrant
75. Noe Valley Ministry

Places to Eat & Drink:

5. RNM
6. Cha Cha Cha
7. Kan Zaman
8. Citrus Club
9. Axum Café
10. Rotee
11. Pork Store Café
12. Rosamunde Sausage Grill
13. Café International
14. Milk
15. Aub Zam Zam
16. Club Deluxe
17. Hobson's Choice
18. Magnolia Pub and Brewery
19. Toronado
20. Noc Noc
37. EOS Restaurant
    and Wine Bar
38. Kezar Bar and Restaurant
39. Zazie
40. Crepes on Cole
41. Reverie Café
42. Boulange de Cole Valley
43. Finnegan's Wake
51. Mecca
52. Côte Sud
53. Tangerine
54. Catch
55. Anchor Oyster Bar
56. 2223 Restaurant and Bar
57. Home
58. Samovar
59. Café du Nord
60. Lucky 13

THE HAIGHT

B: 6, 7, 22, 24, 37, 43, 71
Muni N-Judah line to Cole or Stanyan

• SNAPSHOT •

A romanticized vision of ★THE HAIGHT still exists for many who recall its 1960s halcyon days. Flower children, Deadheads, antiwar activism, and sexual freedom

defined San Francisco and "the Haight-Ashbury." Tourists in search of that past will find "summer of love" and "Hashbury" flashbacks immortalized in neighborhood psychedelic shops, tie-dye outlets, and souvenir stores. But hippies have long been replaced by street urchins asking for cigarettes and change, and flower power has become spending power. This new **Haight** reflects the neighborhood's most recent revival. In the late 1800s, the area bustled with prosperous Victorian-era residents, but declined from the 1920s till its sixties apogee, when Janis Joplin lived at 122 Lyon and Graham Nash at 731 Buena Vista. The 1970s saw another downturn, with abandoned buildings, a homeless population, and growing crime. But the landscape has evolved, thanks to renewed gentrification dating from the 1980s. A commercial sector

dominates "Upper Haight," with vintage clothing boutiques, international restaurants, brunch cafés, and music shops. The more diverse "Lower Haight" stretches from Divisadero east and is lined with coffeehouses, funky bars, and underground record stores.

PLACES TO SEE
Landmarks:

When hippies claimed the corner of **Haight and Ashbury**

(1) in 1967, it became the crossroads of the world's antiestablishment, antiwar, pro-love movement, and rock bands like the Jefferson Airplane made this block their home. But not much is left of those high times, as evidenced by the Gap on one corner and Ben & Jerry's on another. Visitors can still see the **Grateful Dead House (2)** *(710 Ashbury St.)* (now a private residence), where Jerry Garcia and the band bunked in the sixties. Nearby **Buena Vista Park (3)** *(Haight St. and Buena Vista E. and W.)*, another hippie haven, dates from 1867 and was the first city park. John McLaren of Golden Gate Park fame supervised forestation of its approximately 37 acres; its slope, at 589 feet, offers views across the city.

Arts & Entertainment:

Eight independent film fanatics banded together in 1980 to open **Red Vic Movie House (4)** *(1727 Haight St., 415-668-3994, www.redvicmoviehouse.com)*. It now features indie, cult, and second-run big-name flicks, as well as comfy couches and organic refreshments.

PLACES TO EAT & DRINK
Where to Eat:

RNM (5) ($$) *(598 Haight St., 415-551-7900, www.rnm restaurant.com)* serves up small plates of French- and Italian-influenced American cuisine sans attitude and with enough ingenuity to outshine many upscale counterparts. Order a pre-meal sangria and pray for a seat (it's first come, first served, no reservations) at popular **Cha Cha Cha (6) ($)** *(1801 Haight St., 415-386-7670, www.cha3.com)*. Latin and Caribbean tapas are served in a festive atmosphere. There's a party every night at **Kan Zaman (7) ($)** *(1793 Haight St., 415-751-9656)*. Belly dancers take center stage, hookah smoke fills the air, and the tasty Mediterranean menu is almost an afterthought. Lines wrap the waiting area at **Citrus Club (8) ($)** *(1790 Haight St., 415-387-6366)* for soups and heaping Asian-style noodle dishes. **Axum Café (9) ($)** *(698 Haight St., 415-252-7912, www.axumcafe.com)* is known for perfectly spiced Ethiopian fare. Enjoy curries, wraps, vegan dishes, and more amid posters of Bollywood superstars at **Rotee (10) ($)** *(400 Haight St., 415-552-8309, www.roteesf.com)*. Getting over a Saturday night bender? **Pork Store Café (11) ($)** *(1451 Haight St., 415-864-6981)* comes to the rescue with eggs, bacon, hash browns, biscuits, and pork chops. Sample chicken sausage smoked with cherries, duck sausage with figs, and other combos at **Rosamunde Sausage Grill (12) ($)** *(545 Haight St., 415-437-6851)*. Seating is limited, so be prepared to take your sausage for a walk. **Café International (13) ($)** *(508 Haight St., 415-552-7390)* offers flavorful food and one of the friendliest environments in the Haight.

Bars & Nightlife:

Twenty-somethings crowd **Milk (14)** *(1840 Haight St., 415-387-6455, www.milksf.com)* for its steady rotation of DJs blasting house, hip-hop, soul, and funk. Back when local legend Bruno Mooshei ruled **Aub Zam Zam (15)** *(1633 Haight St., 415-861-2545)*, he ousted patrons for improper etiquette, such as ordering a vodka rather than a gin martini. Bruno passed away in 2000, and though the "Bogie with Chesterfield" ambience remains, the bartenders will let you choose your own drink. **Club Deluxe (16)** *(1511 Haight St., 415-552-6949, www.clubdeluxesf.com)*, another throwback, maintains its fifties style with live jazz, swing, and bossa nova. Dip into the Caribbean at **Hobson's Choice (17)** *(1601 Haight St., 415-621-5859, www.hobsonschoice.com)*, a Victorian punch house serving cocktails fashioned from over 70 kinds of rum. **Magnolia Pub and Brewery (18)** *(1398 Haight St., 415-864-7468, www.magnolia pub.com)*, the neighborhood's only brewpub, offers hand-crafted ales and farm-fresh twists on pub cuisine. Newer sister hotspot **The Alembic** *(1725 Haight St., 415-666-0822,*

www.alembicbar.com) serves small plates accompanied by artisan brews and classic cocktails. The Lower Haight's best beer bar, **Toronado (19)** *(547 Haight St., 415-863-2276, www.toronado.com)*, serves local brews and Belgian imports. New York's East Village circa 1984 takes on Dalí-esque touches at **Noc Noc (20)** *(557 Haight St., 415-861-5811)*, with industrial décor and black light.

WHERE TO SHOP

La Rosa Vintage (21) *(1711 Haight St., 415-668-3744)* takes vintage to new levels with exquisite formal attire from the 1920s to 1970s. Villains (22) *(1672 Haight St., 415-626-5939, www.villainssf.com)* caters to skaters, alt-rockers, and hip-hop folk with labels like Paul Frank and Obey. Upscale **Villains Vault** *(1653 Haight St., 415-864-7727)* carries G-Star and Earnest Sewn. Held Over (23) *(1543 Haight St., 415-864-0818)* is a treasure-trove of vintage clothes, including men's shirts and women's cocktail dresses. Behind the Post Office (24) *(1510 Haight St., 415-861-2507)* carries one-of-a-kind fashions by local designers. Charmingly eclectic Doe (25) *(629A Haight St., 415-558-8588, www.doe-sf.com)* offers unique gifts, greeting cards, clothing, books, and more. Saucy Piedmont Boutique (26) *(1452 Haight St., 415-864-8075, www.pied montsf.com)* features boas, bustiers, wigs, and drag queen frocks. What better spot than the Haight for Vancouver-based John Fluevog Shoes (27) *(1697 Haight St., 415-436-9784, www.fluevog.com)* to promote funky, chunky shoes and peace-and-love vibes? Gloomy Bears, Dunnies, Kubricks, Icebots—Kidrobot

(28) *(1512 Haight St., 415-487-9000, www.kid robot.com)* is a hit with kids and adults alike. Premier independent Booksmith (29) *(1644 Haight St., 415-863-8688, www.booksmith.com)* is known for its array of carefully selected new titles. One of the last bastions of free-thinking Haight, Bound Together Book Collective (30) *(1369 Haight St., 415-431-8355)* stocks anarchist and conspiracy literature, history titles, and more. Looking for that Indian sitar classic? Rare punk rock first pressing? Amazing Amoeba Music (31) *(1855 Haight St., 415-831-1200, www.amoebamusic.com)* offers the widest selection of new and used records, CDs, and tapes in the city. Furnish your pad with far-out retro items from Other Shop (32) *(327 Divisadero St., 415-621-5424)*. Hit Happy Trails (33) *(1728 Haight St., 415-831-2264, www.shophappy trails.com)* for Western kitsch, Sigmund Freud bobble-heads, tiki trinkets, and more. Free Bazooka bub-blegum with purchase.

WHERE TO STAY

Innkeeper Sami Sunchild keeps the sixties spirit alive at Red Victorian Bed, Breakfast, & Art (34) ($$) *(1665 Haight St., 415-864-1978, www.redvic.com)*, offering a "Flower Child Room," "Summer of Love Room," and more. Enjoy coffee and sandwiches in its **Peace Café ($)**. Elegant Stanyan Park Hotel (35) ($$) *(750 Stanyan St., 415-751-1000, www.stanyanpark.com)*, across from Golden Gate Park *(see page 153)*, features rooms with full baths and afternoon tea.

COLE VALLEY

B: 6, 37, 43
Muni N-Judah line to Carl & Cole

• SNAPSHOT •

Step over the southern boundary of Haight Street, and the world matures. Young families, nine-to-fivers, and a sprinkling of students fill side-by-side rows of houses. But Cole Valley's main draw is its lineup of inviting cafés and restaurants, a tranquil respite from the weekend throngs of the Haight.

PLACES TO SEE
Landmarks:

Cole Valley offers appealing options for strolling. Try an afternoon walk up Belgrave Street for panoramic views (considered among the city's best) from atop 650-foot **Tank Hill (36)** *(overlooking Twin Peaks Blvd.)*, site of a water supply tank from 1894 to 1957.

PLACES TO EAT & DRINK
Where to Eat:

One of San Francisco's original Asian fusion establishments, **EOS Restaurant and Wine Bar (37) ($$)** *(901 Cole St., 415-566-3063, www.eossf.com)* is a valley institution. Shiitake mushroom dumplings, green curry coconut prawns, and other plates are paired with over 200 wines. Its more relaxed wine bar next door serves the same menu. **Kezar Bar and Restaurant (38) ($)** *(900 Cole St., 415-681-7678)* is an inviting neighborhood spot. Grab a microbrew and peruse early 1900s photos on the walls. The menu, including mac'n'cheese and steamed mussels, surpasses expectations. Cole Valley descends on **Zazie (39) ($)** *(941 Cole St., 415-564-5332, www.zaziesf.com)* for weekend brunch, with residents vying for patio spots when the sun is out. Try the gingerbread pancakes. **Crepes on Cole (40) ($)** *(100 Carl St., 415-664-1800)* also fills up with brunchers seeking sweet and savory crêpes. **Reverie Café (41) ($)** *(848 Cole St., 415-242-0200)* stands out for espresso drinks. Patrons play chess and backgammon and keep the café's small bookshelf stocked. Part of the Boulangerie Bay Bread Group chain, bakery and patisserie **Boulange de Cole Valley (42) ($)** *(1000 Cole St., 415-242-2442, www.baybread.com/cole.php)* is the perfect spot to people watch.

Bars & Nightlife:

Untrendy **Finnegan's Wake (43)** *(937 Cole St., 415-731-6119)* adds a dash of salt to the Cole Valley café lifestyle. Old-timers unwind with a game of pool or a summer barbecue on the patio.

WHERE TO SHOP

Two merchants have teamed up to create one of the best Cole Valley shopping spots at egg + Urban Mercantile (44) *(85 Carl St., 415-564-2248, www.urbanmercantile.com)*, where you'll discover unique housewares, ceramics, gifts, and stationery items. Stumasa Unfinished Furniture (45) *(515 Frederick St., 415-759-1234, www.stumasa.com)* stocks ready-to-finish bookcases, dressers, and tables; environmentally-friendly paints and stains; and funky accessories.

WHERE TO STAY

Cheery Carl Hotel (46) ($) *(198 Carl St., 415-661-5679, http://carlhotel.citysearch.com/)* offers 28 rooms, a peaceful patio, and easy downtown access.

THE CASTRO

B: 24, 33
F-line streetcar
Muni trains K, L, M, and T-Third to Castro St. Station

● SNAPSHOT ●

TOP PICK!

Openly gay ★**CASTRO** struts its stuff with rainbow flags, parades, niche bookstores, and bars with names like Moby Dick. It's hard to imagine the humble roots of this now-vibrant area. The former Eureka Valley was transformed from farmland to residential neighborhood in the late 1800s, when the Market Street Railway linked it to downtown. Scandinavian immigrants and blue-collar Irish populated the area, built Victorian homes, and opened businesses. In the late 1960s and early 1970s, working-class families left for the suburbs. An influx of gays and lesbians, with some spillover from the Haight-Ashbury, purchased the old Victorians and named the district after its main thoroughfare. This burgeoning

neighborhood united after the 1978 assassination of gay San Francisco supervisor Harvey Milk and continued to bond with the onslaught of the AIDS epidemic. Today's gay and lesbian community includes a growing number of families with kids.

PLACES TO SEE

Landmarks:

Harvey Milk Plaza (47) *(Castro and Market Sts.)*, marked by a 20- by 30-foot rainbow flag, commemorates supervisor Milk, who, along with mayor George Moscone, was assassinated at City Hall in 1978 by former supervisor Dan White. White was charged with manslaughter following a trial made famous by its "Twinkie Defense" (junk food was said to have contributed to the depressed White's breakdown). A "White Night Riot" ensued, led by gays and supporters; they set the City Hall lobby and police cars ablaze. Nearby, 15 granite pillars of **Pink Triangle Park and Memorial (48)** *(Market, Castro, and 17th Sts., www.pinktrianglepark.net)* honor the estimated 15,000 lesbians, gays, bisexuals, and transgenders imprisoned and killed during the Nazi era.

Arts & Entertainment:

The Spanish Renaissance **Castro Theatre (49)** *(429 Castro St., 415-621-6120, www.thecastrotheatre.com)* is one of the last operating 1920s movie palaces in the U.S. Old classics and indie films are shown on one mammoth screen; shows begin with an organist at a Wurlitzer that rises from the orchestra pit.

Kids:

Randall Museum (50) *(199 Museum Way, 415-554-9600, www.randallmuseum.org)* is set in a 16-acre park with Bay views. This hands-on museum includes a theater, greenhouse, and arts and ceramics studios.

PLACES TO EAT & DRINK
Where to Eat:

Don't miss **Mecca (51) ($$$)** *(2029 Market St., 415-621-7000, www.sfmecca.com)*, celebrated for swank décor, live DJs, and fresh Kumamoto oysters. Another hot spot: French bistro **Côte Sud (52) ($$)** *(4238 18th St., 415-255-6565, www.cotesudsf.com)*, featuring a prix fixe menu, enclosed terrace, and over 180 wines. Serving Pan-Asian cuisine, **Tangerine (53) ($$)** *(3499 16th St., 415-626-1700, www. tangerinesf.com)* leads the short list of local eateries that excel at brunch and dinner. Seafood, not surprisingly, is the priority at **Catch (54) ($$)** *(2362 Market St., 415-431-5000, www.catchsf.com)*. Dine outdoors on the heated patio or inside nearer live piano jazz. The fish, sans scene, lures locals to an upbeat storefront setting at **Anchor Oyster Bar (55) ($$)** *(579 Castro St., 415-431-3990)*. American cuisine and Sunday brunch at **2223 Restaurant and Bar (56) ($-$$)** *(2223 Market St., 415-431-0692, www.2223 restaurant.com)* have made a name for this upbeat spot. **Home (57) ($)** *(2100 Market St., 415-503-0333, www.home-sf.com)* also features an American menu with choices like Niman Ranch pot roast and banana bread pudding. Serene **Samovar (58) ($)** *(498 Sanchez St., 415-626-4700, www.samovartea.com)* pairs more than 100 teas with eclectic treats, such as Masala chai with cherry oat scones.

Bars & Nightlife:

Done in deep reds and dark woods, **Café du Nord (59)** *(2170 Market St, 415-861-5016, www.cafedunord.com)* evokes its former speakeasy heyday. Today's patrons enjoy live music, from punk to jazz to swing. **Lucky 13 (60)** *(2140 Market St., 415-487-1313)* is one of San Francisco's few true hard rockin' bars, with German beers on tap. The Castro takes a different turn at **Swirl on Castro (61)** *(572 Castro St., 415-864-2262, www. swirloncastro.com)*, a wine bar offering small production labels, plus spirits, glassware, and related gifts. The 1972 opening of **Twin Peaks Tavern (62)** *(401 Castro St., 415-864-9470, www.twinpeakstavern.com)* was a community milestone; it was the first gay bar with full windows. This friendly tavern now attracts an older, mostly gay clientele. A younger crowd stakes out red-light lounge **Bar on Castro (63)** *(456 Castro St., 415-626-7220)*. Well-heeled locals flirt while nursing Long Island iced teas. Neighborhood bar **Moby Dick (64)** *(4049 18th St., 415-861-1199, www.mobydicksf.com)* has been around for over 25 years. This is the place for pool, pinball, and touch-screen trivia. The Castro croons at **The Mint Karaoke Lounge (65)** *(1942 Market St., 415-626-4726, www.themint.net)*. Go ahead, get in touch with your inner *American Idol*. Soft lighting, softer couches, and a retro urban interior attract gays and straights to **Amber (66)** *(718 14th St., 415-626-7827)*. Chill DJs add to the vibe. Note: Smoking is allowed, so the air can get thick.

WHERE TO SHOP

Venerable **Cliff's Variety (67)** *(479 Castro St., 415-431-5365, www.cliffsvariety.com)* fills its aisles with everything from craft supplies and Art Deco doorknobs to tiaras and toy rubber insects. Clever gifts and houseware items, Zen cat statues, and Elvis tape dispensers abound **Under One Roof (68)** *(549 Castro St., 415-503-2300, www.underoneroof.org)*; proceeds go toward agencies that provide HIV/AIDS support. **A Different Light Bookstore (69)** *(489 Castro St., 415-431-0891, www.adlbooks.com)* is packed with gay, lesbian, bisexual, and transgender books, magazines, movies, greeting cards, and calendars; it also hosts author events.

WHERE TO STAY

The 1909 Edwardian **Parker Guest House (70) ($$)** *(520 Church St., 415-621-3222, www.parkerguesthouse.com)* offers well-appointed rooms (most with private baths), a library with fireplace and piano, breakfast, and afternoon wine socials. Comfy **Willows Inn (71) ($-$$)** *(710 14th St., 415-431-4770, www.willowssf.com)* provides antique-filled accommodations with sinks, shared baths/showers, robes, breakfast, cocktails, and more. **Inn on Castro (72) ($-$$)** *(321 Castro St., 415-861-0321, www.innoncastro.com)*, another restored Edwardian, has eight spacious rooms and suites, most with private baths, plus self-catering apartments. Rates include full breakfast and evening brandy.

NOE VALLEY

B: 24, 35, 37, 48
Muni J-Church line

• SNAPSHOT •

Noe Valley was once filled with farms and ranches, including Rancho San Miguel, owned by Don José de Jesús Noé, the last mayor of Yerba Buena, the Mexican village that became San Francisco. In 1906, the valley began attracting victims of the city's great earthquake.

Displaced residents erected rows of Victorians and Edwardians that today house affluent young professionals and families, many of whom cashed in during the dot-com boom. Most traffic runs along 24th Street and up Church, where locals linger over brunch or stroll the modest shopping strip.

PLACES TO SEE
Landmarks:

Rising more than 900 feet over Noe Valley, **Twin Peaks (73)** *(Twin Peaks Blvd.)*, the city's second highest hills after Mt. Davidson, afford views of the Golden Gate Bridge, Bay, and skyline. Hope for a clear day, as the peaks are often enveloped in fog, and don't forget a jacket; the wind is brisk. During the 1906 post-earthquake conflagrations, which lasted for three days, every fire hydrant in the vicinity went dry except the **Golden Fire Hydrant (74)** *(20th and Church Sts. across from Mission Dolores Park)*. It gets a fresh coat of gold paint every April 18.

Arts & Entertainment:

Artists like Warren Zevon, Culture Clash comedy troupe, and Scottish fiddler Alasdair Fraser have performed for the Noe Valley Music Series at **Noe Valley Ministry (75)** *(1021 Sanchez St., 415-454-5238, www.noevalleymusicseries.com)*, a 110-year-old Victorian landmark.

PLACES TO EAT & DRINK
Where to Eat:
Firefly (76) ($$) *(4288 24th St., 415-821-7652, www.fireflyrestaurant.com)* is a cozy spot punctuated with art and a mix of home-style cuisines, from Asian to Mediterranean to Californian. **Bistro 1689 (77) ($$)** *(1689 Church St., 415-550-8298, www.bistro1689.com)* sparks a buzz for flawless French-Cal creations, from papaya-avocado salad to roast hen-of-the-woods mushroom.

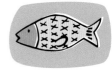

Pescheria (78) ($$) *(1708 Church St., 415-647-3200, www.pescheria-sf.com)* emphasizes seafood and pastas.

Dine on the patio when the weather is warm. Tempting **La Ciccia (79) ($-$$)** *(291 30th St., 415-550-8114, www.laciccia.com)* serves Sardinian dishes like braised tuna with tomato and mint. The brunch line is longest at **Chloe's Café (80) ($)** *(1399 Church St., 415-648-4116)*; half the neighborhood awaits its scrambled eggs and pecan pancakes. Brunch at **Pomelo (81) ($)** *(1793 Church St., 415-285-2257, www.pomelosf.com)* is all over the map, from cold buckwheat noodle salad to baked cheddar-jalapeño polenta. Whether high tea, Queen's tea, or "wee tea," everyone loves **Lovejoy's Tea Room (82) ($)** *(1351 Church St., 415-648-5895, www.lovejoystearoom.com)*, for its mismatched china and scrumptious scones. **Mitchell's Ice Cream (83) ($)** *(688 San Jose Ave., 415-648-2300, www.mitchellsicecream.com)*, an institution since 1953, features flavors ranging from

strawberry and vanilla to Kahlua Mocha Cream, *buko* (baby coconut), and *ube* (purple yam).

Bars & Nightlife:

It may resemble a too-trendy lounge, but **Bliss Bar (84)** *(4026 24th St., 415-826-6200, www.blissbarsf.com)* is actually a low-key spot with jamming DJs, friendly bar staff, and specialty drinks. Want a more casual vibe? Try Irish pub **The Dubliner (85)** *(3838 24th St., 415-826-2279)* for stouts, TV sports, and sociable patrons.

Cute but claustrophobic Ambiance (86) *(3985 and 3989 24th St., 415-647-7144, www.ambiancesf.com)* is wall-to-wall dresses, tops, bags, and shoes. Nisa (87) *(3789 24th St., 415-920-9149, www.nisasf.com)*, Arabic for "woman," a clothing shop run by five area women, leans toward edgy with striking colors and off-beat cuts. The staggering selection of new and used titles at Phoenix Books (88) *(3850 24th St., 415-821-3477)* is hard to resist. Cover to Cover Booksellers (89) *(1307 Castro St., 415-282-8080)* is such a beloved Noe Valley institution, residents committed to buying books here in order to save it from going out of business a while back. Colorful Wink SF (90) *(4107 24th St., 415-401-8881)* is a variety store minus "garden variety" items. Instead, expect sushi pens, Tofu Robot T-shirts, Japanese toys, and

Angry Little Girls accessories. The Ark Toy Company (91) *(3845 24th St., 415-821-1257, www.thearktoys.com)* carries high-quality educational toys, books, board games, science kits, and "green" toys, such as blocks made of reclaimed wood.

WHERE TO STAY

A local family offers private accommodations at the Hidden Cottage (92) ($$) *(1186 Noe St., 415-282-4492, www.hidden-cottage.com/hidden.html)*, a bougainvillea-adorned Victorian home with a queen-size bed, deck, and garden.

"No city invites the heart to come to life as San Francisco does…."

—*William Saroyan*

chapter 9

DECO GHETTO
THE MISSION
BERNAL HEIGHTS
POTRERO HILL/DOGPATCH

Places to See:

1. The Center
2. Lincart
17. Mission Dolores
18. Mission Dolores Park
19. Balmy Alley
20. Precita Eyes Mural Arts
    and Visitors Center
21. Galeria de la Raza
22. Lost Art Salon
23. Roxie Cinema/Film Center
54. Bernal Heights Park
55. Holly Park
71. Vermont Street
72. Anchor Brewing Company
73. San Francisco Center
    for the Book

Places to Eat & Drink:

3. Zuni Cafe
4. DeLessio Market & Bakery
5. Espetus Churrascaria
6. Destino
7. Sushi Zone
8. Cav Wine Bar
9. Hôtel Biron
10. Orbit Room
11. Martuni's
12. Zeitgeist
24. La Taqueria
25. Pancho Villa Taqueria
26. Limón
27. Range
28. Delfina
29. Slow Club
30. Dosa
31. Bissap Baobab
32. Foreign Cinema
33. Atlas Café
34. Café Gratitude
35. Tartine Bakery
36. St. Francis Fountain
    & Candy Store
37. El Rio
38. Nihon Whisky Lounge
39. Levende Lounge
40. Amnesia
41. Dalva
42. Lexington Club
43. Elixir

Where to Shop:

Where to Stay:

"The cool, grey city of love."

—*George Sterling*

DECO GHETTO

B: 6, 26, 49, 71
F-line streetcar, Muni trains to Van Ness Ave. Station

• SNAPSHOT •

Though not yet listed on major maps, an emerging neighborhood dubbed Deco Ghetto has taken root along the Upper Market corridor from Franklin to Guerrero, and south down Valencia to 14th Street. The name comes from the Art Deco design stores that dot the area, but Deco Ghetto is more than antique dealers and book and music purveyors. The area is expanding with new wine bars, live jazz lounges, and French bistros. While lacking true community, the district is considered a shopping and entertainment destination, in keeping with its old nickname, "The Hub."

PLACES TO SEE
Landmarks:
The Center (1) *(1800 Market St., 415-865-5555, www.sfcenter.org)*, the San Francisco Lesbian Gay Bisexual Transgender (LGBT) Center, offers health and wellness programs and arts and cultural activities.

Arts & Entertainment:

Lincart (2) *(1632-C Market St., 415-503-1981, www.lincart.com)* offers an expansive space in which to view contemporary, sometimes challenging works of art. The gallery also deals in some modern works by Warhol, Arbus, and others.

PLACES TO EAT & DRINK
Where to Eat:

Even after over 20 years, **Zuni Cafe (3) ($-$$)** *(1658 Market St., 415-552-2522)* still gets a buzz going. Its two spacious floors fill with locals seeking fresh-shucked oysters, Caesar salad, and roasted chicken. **DeLessio Market & Bakery (4) ($)** *(1695 Market St., 415-552-5559, www.delessiomarket.com),* more a takeout than a sit-down spot, dishes out basics like mac'n'cheese and desserts like bread pudding. Meat eaters will find paradise on a skewer at Brazilian style **Espetus Churrascaria (5) ($$)** *(1686 Market St., 415-552-8792, www.espetus.com).* The warm glow at **Destino (6) ($$)** *(1815 Market St., 415-552-4451, www.destinosf.com)* befits its friendly ambience and shared small-plates menu, including seafood *ceviche* and grilled Portobello/eggplant *empanadas.* Join the line to dine at tiny **Sushi Zone (7) ($-$$)** *(1815 Market St., 415-621-1114).* The rewards are robust rolls like *unagi* papaya or dishes like striped bass with mango.

Bars & Nightlife:

Elegant **Cav Wine Bar (8)** *(1666 Market St, 415-437-1770, www.cavwinebar.com)* pours more than 300 wines by the bottle and 40 by the glass. **Hôtel Biron (9)** *(45 Rose St., 415-703-0403, www.hotelbiron.com)*, with its European touches, is an inviting setting for sipping wine and snacking on olives and cheese. Sip specialty cocktails at *Jetsons*-style tables inside **Orbit Room (10)** *(1900 Market St., 415-252-9525)*. Floor-to-ceiling windows lend views outside. San Francisco lets its hair down at **Martuni's (11)** *(4 Valencia St., 415-241-0205, www.martunis.citysearch.com)*. Martinis are shaken and stirred and patrons belt out show tunes at the piano bar. A biker aesthetic and rockin' jukebox complement the Bloody Marys and draught beers served at **Zeitgeist (12)** *(199 Valencia St., 415-255-7505, www.zeitgeist.citysearch.com)*.

WHERE TO SHOP

Another Time (13) *(1710 Market St., 415-553-8900, www.anothertimesf.com)* turns back the clock with home furnishings from the 1930s to the 1960s. Bell'occhio (14) *(8 Brady St., 415-864-4048, www.bellocchio.com)* imports gift items from a variety of French ateliers, including candles, perfumes, artisan chocolates, and teas. Gourmet foodies browse Yum (15) *(1750 Market St., 415-626-9866, www.yumfoods.com)* for specialty items like Strawberry Marshmallow Fluff and neon-hued soft drinks from around the world. Real-world wanderers and armchair travelers alike navigate the aisles at Get Lost Travel Books (16) *(1825 Market St., 415-437-0529, www.getlostbooks.com)*.

THE MISSION

B: 9, 12, 14, 22, 27, 33, 49
Muni J-Church line
BART to 16th or 24th St. Stations

• SNAPSHOT •

Named after Mission Dolores, the city's oldest Spanish mission, the Mission District (and especially Mission Street), is an amalgam of *taquerías*, Salvadorian *pupuserías*, thrift stores, and dive bars. A concentration of cultural outlets lies along 24th Street between Mission and Potrero, in *El Corazon de la Misione*, "Heart of the Mission." The Mission's other thoroughfare, Valencia Street between 16th and 24th, is a different story. Relatively cheap rents drew artists, musicians, and bohemians here in the 1970s and 1980s, while last decade's dot-com boom attracted über-trendy professionals who gobbled up Valencia real estate and opened funky cafés, hip bars, tapas lounges, galleries, boutiques, and underground book and music shops.

PLACES TO SEE
Landmarks:

Mission Dolores (17) *(3321 16th St., 415-621-8203, www.missiondolores.org)*, a 200-year-old adobe chapel next door to the towering **Mission Dolores Basilica** is San Francisco's oldest building. Services are held here every June 29 commemorating the Mission's (and the city's) founding in 1776. The chapel features frescoes and hand-painted altars from Mexico. You'll also find a small museum, heirloom plant garden, and a cemetery you may recall from the Hitchcock movie *Vertigo*. On any given sunny weekend, locals pack picnic baskets and leash their pups for an outing at **Mission Dolores Park (18)** *(bordered by 18th, Dolores, 20th, and Church Sts.)*. The park screens outdoor movies in summer *(www.doloresparkmovie.org)* and is a venue for performances by the **San Francisco Mime Troupe** *(415-285-1717, www.sfmt.org)*.

Arts & Entertainment:

The Mission is home to dozens of murals, many with political or social messages, painted on buildings, fences, and garage doors. The most colorful line **Balmy Alley (19)** *(bordered by Treat Ave. and 24th, Harrison, and 25th Sts.)*. The mural movement dates from the 1970s; today, nonprofit **Precita Eyes Mural Arts and Visitors Center (20)** *(2981 24th St., 415-285-2287, www.precitaeyes.org)* promotes these unique works of art with tours, mural maps, workshops, art supply sales, and tours. **Galeria de la Raza (21)** *(2857 24th St., 415-826-8009, www.galeriadelaraza.org)* is a nexus for San Francisco's Latino arts, with exhibits, performances, films, and multimedia works. Original works by unknown or "lost" artists take precedence at **Lost Art Salon (22)** *(245 S. Van Ness Ave., 415-861-1530, www.lostartsalon.com)*. Pieces date to 1900 and include Modernist, Arts and Crafts, and other movements. The 1913 **Roxie Cinema/Film Center (23)** *(3117 16th St., 415-863-1087, www.roxie.com)*, known for edgy offerings, shows more documentaries than any other theater in the country. It's also a film studies facility for the New College of California.

PLACES TO EAT & DRINK
Where to Eat:

Traditional *taquerias* and *papuserías* dominate the Mission's culinary landscape. **La Taqueria (24) ($)** *(2889 Mission St., 415-285-7117)* is always a contender in the "city's best *taqueria*" debate. The in-your-face lighting and cafeteria setting at lively **Pancho Villa Taqueria (25) ($)** *(3071 16th St., 415-864-8840, www.panchovillasf.com)* are redeemed by overstuffed burritos and mariachi musicians. Peruvian classics like *ceviche* mixed with Nuevo-Latino fusion have catapulted **Limón (26) ($$)** *(524 Valencia St, 415-252-0918, www.limon-sf.com)* into the limelight. Funky décor and a seasonal Am-Cal menu make **Range (27) ($$)** *(842 Valencia St., 415-282-8283, www.rangesf.com)* one of the strip's hottest tables. **Delfina (28) ($$)** *(3621 18th St., 415-552-4055, www.delfinasf.com)* serves trattoria-style cuisine to the upwardly hip. **Slow Club (29) ($$)** *(2501 Mariposa St., 415-241-9390, www.slowclub.com)* turns up the beat as it churns out plates of American fare, like pan-seared coho salmon with apple cider-braised Treviso, roasted carrots, golden raisins, and herbs. **Dosa (30) ($)** *(995 Valencia St., 415-642-3672, www.dosasf.com)* deserves accolades for savory, South Indian-style crepes. **Bissap Baobab (31) ($)** *(2323 Mission St., 415-826-9287, www.bissapbaobab.com/)*, with homemade ginger cocktails and Senegalese cuisine, adds another dimension to Mission dining. Enjoy a changing Cal-Med menu and film classics in the outdoor courtyard at **Foreign Cinema (32) ($$)** *(2534 Mission St., 415-648-7600, www.foreign cinema.com)*. Then step inside its **László Bar** for nightly DJs. More than just a lunch spot, **Atlas Café (33) ($)** *(3049 20th St., 415-648-1047, www.atlascafe.net)* is a social center with a patio and live jazz, blues, or bluegrass Thursdays and Saturdays. Healthy eats include baked beet and kale sandwiches, corn chowder, and vegan pizza. **Café Gratitude (34) ($)** *(2400 Harrison St., 415-824-4652, www.withthecurrent.com/cafe.html)* serves raw comfort foods. Communal seating and menu items like "I Am Elated" make this an "only-in-San Francisco" experience. For baked goods, head to **Tartine Bakery (35) ($)** *(600 Guerrero St., 415-487-2600, www.tartinebakery.com)*, so popular it has its own cookbook. Its **Bar Tartine ($$)** *(561 Valencia St, 415-487-1600)* offers a full menu. **St. Francis Fountain & Candy Store (36) ($)** *(2801 24th St., 415-826-4200)*, dating to 1918, serves sundaes and ice cream sodas.

Bars & Nightlife:

El Rio (37) *(3158 Mission St., 415-282-3325, www.elriosf.com)* livens the Mission with seasonal Sunday salsa parties. DJs spin most nights; local bands are featured on Saturdays. **Nihon Whisky Lounge (38) ($-$$)** *(1779 Folsom St., 415-552-4400, www.nihon-sf.com)* serves Japanese small plates in a chic, low-key setting. The real menu is its list of more than 120 whiskies. Mood lighting and downtempo beats add to the ambience at **Levende Lounge (39)** *(1710 Mission St., 415-864-5585, www.levendesf.com)*. Scarlet-hued **Amnesia (40)** *(853 Valencia St., 415-970-0012, www.amnesiathebar.com)* has an eclectic music calendar, including live bluegrass, DJs, jazz, Gypsy brass, and karaoke. Even when crowded, divey **Dalva (41)** *(3121 16th St., 415-252-7740)* retains a cool neighborhood vibe, thanks to able DJs. Lesbians get into the groove at **Lexington Club (42)** *(3464 19th St., 415-863-2052, www.lexingtonclub.com)*; the club features art by area women. Historic **Elixir (43)** *(3200 16th St., 415-552-1633, www.elixirsf.com)*, established in 1858, has been fully restored, down to its mahogany bar.

WHERE TO SHOP

With two locations, Therapy (44) *(545 Valencia St., 415-861-6213, 541 Valencia St., 415-621-5902)* blends retro and modern furniture with funky clothes, jewelry, and gifts. Dema Grim of Dema (45) *(1038 Valencia St., 415-206-0500, www.godemago.com)* puts a spin on retro '50s, '60s, and '70s classics. Schauplatz (46) *(791 Valencia St., 415-864-5665)*, "the scene," shines with vintage gems from the '60s, and '70s. Fabric8 (47) *(3318 22nd St., 415-647-5888, www.fabric8.com)* features local artists' and designers' work—everything from silk-screened T-shirts to affordable paintings. Pirate supply store 826 Valencia (48) *(826 Valencia St., 415-642-5905, www.826valencia.org)* stocks eye patches, spy glasses, and more. Proceeds go to the **826 Valencia Writing Center** for kids. Established in 1970, Aquarius Records (49) *(1055 Valencia St., 415-647-2272, www.aquarius records.org)*, the city's oldest independent record store, has it all—from indie rock and reggae to bluegrass and found sounds. Science fiction, fantasy, and horror book hounds will find over 14,000 new and used titles at Borderlands Books (50) *(866 Valencia St., 415-824-8203, www.borderlands-books.com)*. It takes tenacity to sift the shelves at Dog Eared Books (51) *(900 Valencia St., 415-282-1901, www.dogearedbooks.com)*, but you might be rewarded with a savvy political satire or rare art book.

WHERE TO STAY

The Inn San Francisco (52) *($-$$) (943 S. Van Ness Ave., 415-641-0188, www.innsf.com)*, boasts antique-filled B&B accommodations, an English garden, rooftop sundeck, and hot tub. Welcoming B&B Noe's Nest (53) *($$) (1257 Guerrero St., 415-821-0751, www.noesnest.com)* has six rooms, including three deluxe apartments.

B: 14, 24, 67

• SNAPSHOT •

Unfazed by waves of young families and first-time home buyers, Bernal Heights clings to old community roots with mom-and-pop shops, dog-friendly parks, neighborhood bars, and just enough alternative flair to make it San Francisco. Sometimes called "Maternal Heights" because of its many lesbian moms, the area is mostly residential, with one lively commercial strip along Cortland Avenue. During the Vietnam War, the neighborhood was called "Red Hill" for the antiwar activists who lived in many of its shared houses. Bernal boomed in the dot-com '90s, when newly moneyed professionals sought its relatively affordable real estate. Funky restaurants and a new wine bar now coexist with old groceries and bookshops, but Bernal has sidestepped over-gentrification.

PLACES TO SEE
Landmarks:
Bernal Heights Park (54) *(Bernal Heights Blvd. at Folsom St. S.)* atop Bernal Hill, affords 360-degree views over the Mission and Noe Valley, to Candlestick Point, and

all the way out to Marin and the Golden Gate Bridge. **Holly Park (55)** *(Park St., Bocana St., and Highland Ave.)* spans over seven acres; it's a favorite for its inviting green expanse and pine, eucalyptus, and olive trees.

PLACES TO EAT & DRINK
Where to Eat:

Japanese-Hawaiian fusion inspires menu choices at **Moki's Sushi and Pacific Grill (56) ($-$$)** *(615 Cortland Ave., 415-970-9336, www.moki sushi.com)*. Try the "drum roll"— snow crab, mango, and mint. Family-run **Angkor Borei (57) ($)** *(3471 Mission St., 415-550-8417, www.cambodiankitchen. com)* has been serving authentic

Cambodian dishes for 20 years; options include *ahmohk*, curry fish mousse served in a banana leaf basket. **Little Nepal (58) ($)** *(925 Cortland St., 415-643-3881, www.littlenepalsf.com)* wins big raves for its Northern Indian and Tibetan offerings, including *momos* and *tandoori* dishes. Diners squeeze into the few tables at **Valentina Ristorante (59) ($-$$)** *(419 Cortland Ave., 415-285-6000)* for Ligurian comfort cuisine and displays of local art. Hipsters make tracks to **Emmy's Spaghetti Shack (60) ($)** *(18 Virginia St., 415-206-2086)* for an artsy vibe and inexpensive eats. DJs spin Thursdays through Saturdays. Alterna-types also like the ambience at American-style **Blue Plate (61) ($$)** *(3218 Mission St., 415-282-6777, www.blueplatesf.com)*, which furnishes its dining and garden areas with found objects.

With comfort foods all the rage, **The Front Porch ($)** *(65 29th St., 415-695-7800, www.thefrontporchsf.com)* has become an instant favorite. Likewise, **Liberty Café (62) ($)** *(410 Cortland Ave., 415-695-1223, www.thelibertycafe.com)* dishes out traditional delights like chicken pot pie. Its **Cottage Bakery** is a wine bar Thursdays through Saturdays. No trek to Bernal Heights is complete without a stop at **MaggieMudd (63) ($)** *(903 Cortland Ave., 415-641-5291, www.maggiemudd.com)* for ice cream. The menu includes milk shakes with names like "Green Hornet" and vegan flavors like "Flyin' Hawaiian."

Bars & Nightlife:

The couple owning **VinoRosso's (64)** *(629 Cortland Ave., 415-647-1268)* serve up *stuzzichini* ("small bites"), and homemade pastas with a primarily Italian wine menu. A vestige of the Bernal Heights of old, **Skip's Tavern (65)** *(453 Cortland Ave., 415-282-3456, www.skipstavern. com)* exudes working class attitude. Marilyn Monroe photos dot the walls and R&B musicians jam most every night. Lesbian-owned **Wild Side West (66)** *(424 Cortland Ave., 415-647-3099)*, on the block since 1962, opens its sculpture garden and divey interior to a friendly mixed crowd.

WHERE TO SHOP

Get a pre-brunch bargain-hunting fix Sunday mornings at Alemany Flea Market (67) *(100 Alemany Blvd.,*

415-647-2043). You'll find more antiques and vintage clothes than junk. Red Hill Books (68) *(401 Cortland Ave., 415-648-5331)* recently expanded to accommodate its stock of mostly secondhand titles. It also hosts author events and art openings. Heartfelt (69) *(436 Cortland Ave., 415-648-1380, www.heartfeltsf.com)* is gift central, with knickknacks, toys, funky jewelry, tiny purses, and home items. Gift-wrapping is free. Chloe's Closet (70) *(451A Cortland Ave., 415-642-3300, www.chloescloset.com)* buys, sells, and trades kids' clothes, from newborn to age six, plus maternity wear. Its 443 Cortland location features toys and books.

"East is East, and West
is San Francisco."

—*O. Henry*

POTRERO HILL/DOGPATCH

B: 10, 19, 22, 48, 53
Muni T-Third line along 3rd St.

● SNAPSHOT ●

Potrero Hill celebrates the bohemian lifestyle with outdoor cafés, offbeat bars, and quirky shops. The neighborhood enjoys more sunshine than any other, boasts some of the city's best views, and has recently developed buzzworthy nightlife. Settled in the late 1800s largely by European immigrants who worked in shipbuilding and other industries, Potrero was invaded a century later by alterna-types seeking cheap housing and old Victorians to restore. Adjacent "Dogpatch," along 3rd Street between 16th and Cesar Chavez, is named for packs of dogs that once roamed here. Like Potrero Hill, Dogpatch began as a hub for industry and a home for an immigrant population; it's staging a comeback following decades of decline.

PLACES TO SEE
Landmarks:

The real "crookedest street" in San Francisco is **Vermont Street (71)** *(bet. 20th and 22nd)*. It's not as picturesque as famous Lombard *(see page 33)* and there are fewer hairpin turns, but it is steeper. **Anchor Brewing Company (72)** *(1705 Mariposa St., 415-863-8350, www.anchorbrewing.com)*, dating from 1896, offers one tour and tasting each weekday afternoon. The tour is free, but reservations are a must. Call at least a month in advance.

Arts & Entertainment:

San Francisco Center for the Book (73) *(300 De Haro St., 415-565-0545, www.sfcb.org)* celebrates the history and art of books and bookmaking with classes, events, and exhibits.

PLACES TO EAT & DRINK
Where to Eat:

Voted one of the city's best independent coffeehouses, **Farley's (74) ($)** *(1315 18th St., 415-648-1545, www.farleyscoffee.com)* features live music and exhibits by local artists. The crimson décor at **Baraka (75) ($$)** *(288 Connecticut St., 415-255-0387, www.barakasf.net)* sets the stage for large and small Moroccan and French-Med dishes, such as pistachio-encrusted goat cheese with onion jam and honey. Cozy **Couleur Café (76) ($-$$)** *(300 De Haro St., 415-255-1021, www.couleur*

cafesf.com) entices with French multicultural fare, like duck confit quesadillas with onions, Gruyère, and *crème fraîche*. Locals pack **Aperto Restaurant (77) ($)** *(1434 18th St., 415-252-1625, www.apertosf.com)* for Italian that incorporates fresh organic, seasonal, and local ingredients. **Chez Papa (78) ($$)** *(1401 18th St., 415-255-0387, www.chezpapasf.com)* keeps its atmosphere light, upbeat, and French. Sister eatery **Chez Maman (79) ($$)** *(1453 18th St., 415-824-7166, www.chezmamansf.com)* brings exquisite bistro cuisine to the Potrero. **Goat Hill Pizza (80) ($)** *(300 Connecticut St., 415-641-1440, www.goathill.com)* draws diners for its sourdough crusts and great views. Come Monday for all-you-can-eat "Neighborhood Night."

Bars & Nightlife:

When a main act takes the turntables, **Mighty (81)** *(119 Utah St., 415-762-0151, www.mighty119.com)* fires on all cylinders. The club has an outstanding sound system and a well-coiffed yet unpretentious crowd. **Bottom of the Hill (82)** *(1233 17th St., 415-621-4455, www.bottomofthehill.com)* showcases live local acts, from indie rock to funk. Latin dancers converge at **Café Cocomo (83)** *(650 Indiana St., 415-824-6910, www.cafe cocomo.com)* Thursday and Saturday nights, when salsa sizzles. Lessons are available. Friendly **Sadie's Flying Elephant (84)** *(491 Potrero Ave., 415-551-7988)* has comfy armchairs, pool tables, free popcorn, even a small library. **Jack's Club (85)** *(2545 24th St., 415-641-5371, www.jacks-club.com)* heats up for twice-weekly karaoke and local bands and Saturday night DJs. **Yield Wine Bar**

(86) *(2490 3rd St., 415-401-8984, www.yieldsf.com)* features "green" wines cultivated from organic, biodynamic, and sustainable methods.

WHERE TO SHOP

Dandelion **(87)** *(55 Potrero Ave., 415-436-9500, www.dandelionsf.com)* presents two floors of charming housewares, books, and cards. Independent Christopher's Books **(88)** *(1400 18th St., 415-255-8802)* is one of the most accommodating bookshops in town. Collage Gallery **(89)** *(1345 18th St., 415-282-4401)* offers unique items by 100 area artists as well as furniture and vintage items.

"San Francisco has only one drawback. 'Tis hard to leave."

—Rudyard Kipling

INDEX